OUTDOOR PROJECTS

STEP–BY–STEP

THE LYONS PRESS

Guilford, Connecticut
An imprint of The Globe Pequot Press

PENNY SWIFT & JANEK SZYMANOWSKI

OUTDOOR
PROJECTS

STEP–BY–STEP

The Lyons Press is an imprint of The Globe Pequot Press

10 9 8 7 6 5 4 3 2 1

Design by Geraldine Cupido

Printed and bound in Singapore by Tien Wah Press (PTE) Limited

Reproduction by Hirt and Carter (Cape) Pty Ltd
ISBN 1 59228 029 3.

CONTENTS

■ STONE   14

■ WATER   60

■ BRICK 112

■ WOOD 158

In years to come, climbing plants will overgrow this pergola to provide a shady walk.

INTRODUCTION

FOR HUNDREDS OF YEARS, humankind has created and tended gardens of one sort or another. Some were established primarily to provide food, while others were created as sacred places, or simply developed to provide pleasure. Today there is a vast diversity of garden types and styles. Some are formal, others informal; some are based on established traditional genre, while a huge number are multipurpose areas designed to make the best of the space allowed.

A garden takes many years to establish itself, particularly as it takes time for trees to grow and shrubs to mature. But while plants develop, there is the opportunity to increase the character and function within the entire outdoor space, by adding features that are both practical and attractive. Even if yours is a well-developed garden, you may want to include a path, perhaps a screen wall to give an existing patio privacy, a treehouse or play structure to keep children occupied. A pond will introduce a sense of calm, while a pergola will add a decorative quality. A rustic bench provides somewhere to sit and a planter will allow you to add color to the garden. The options are endless and the materials diverse.

This book presents a selection of projects, of varying degrees of complexity, which may be built from a selection of materials: wood, brick and stone. In addition, it includes a variety of water features and fountains, ponds and pools. Many of the options you will be able to tackle with basic skills. Each project includes a shopping list for materials, as well as tools required for the job so that you can establish what it will cost to construct each feature and make sure you have everything before you start work. An estimated time frame is also provided, as is an indication of the level of skills that may be required – one hammer means that the project is quite simple and straightforward, two that you will need at least some DIY ability, and three that the project you are about to tackle demands some expertise, time and/or patience. These, of course, are just a guideline and will vary, depending not only on soil conditions and how long it takes you to dig holes for foundations, ponds and so on, but also how much assistance you have. Succinct step-by-step photographs accompany each project from start to finish, enabling you to achieve a thoroughly professional look.

PLANNING & DESIGN

PLANNING & DESIGN

Designing a garden can be a daunting task, particularly if you are starting from scratch. Paths, steps and patios form the skeleton of a garden, while walls, fences and hedges contain it and offer an opportunity to divide it. While plants are vital to a garden scheme, structures may also be considered for aesthetic reasons and to make the outdoor area more functional. Ultimately, you should aim for unity and harmony and try to choose materials that will suit the house and blend in with the style of the garden.

TYPE AND STYLE

There are two basic garden types – formal and informal. Likewise, features and structures may also be categorized this way. Garden style, on the other hand, may relate to architecture, a period look, or even a style suggested by a common approach in a certain country or area like Japan or the Mediterranean countries. Certain styles are also often linked to basic garden types. A cottage-style garden, for instance, may be informal, while a garden modelled on meticulously laid out Italian villa gardens will be formal, even if it is not as grand.

Primarily, the layout determines a garden type, but structures and style of planting should also keep with the look. So, too, should the materials for structures or surfacing a garden floor. While steps in a formal garden may follow straight lines and will usually be built from brick, informal staircases will be less rigid, utilizing stone or timber. Timber in a formal garden may be neatly sawn and even painted.

RIGHT *The simple design of this rustic wooden bridge makes it an ideal project for anyone with basic carpentry skills.*

THE PLAN

It does not matter whether you are starting from nothing or simply building features that will improve the look of your garden, sketch the area and draw in walls, buildings, fences and so on, as well as established trees, boulders and other existing features. You will also need to note any sloping ground. Draw the plan to scale. If possible, spend time in the garden, noting sun patterns and prevailing winds and indicate these on the plan. Also mark views and buildings that overlook your property. This will help identify locations for paths, steps, patios, walls, and other structures.

THE LOCATION

One of the most important elements of building a garden structure is choosing the most suitable location. Almost all these projects are permanent structures that cannot be moved, so consider the advantages and disadvantages of each. Try to visualize the finished feature in the site you have chosen, and then reconsider your plan if necessary.

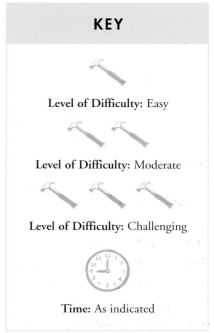

ABOVE *Plan walkways and features so that they blend with and enhance the architectural lines of your home.*

CONSIDER ALL THE OPTIONS

Plans and locations depend almost entirely on individual gardens. For instance, the obvious route for a path may be from the gate to the front door, but if it bisects a lawn, you may prefer it to curve around an existing flower bed or, if the garden is on more than one level, link the path to steps.

The location of a pond depends on local conditions (including soil), gradient of the land, and the existence of rocks and established plants. Areas with natural boulders and secluded corners on lower ground lend themselves to ponds and pools. If the ground slopes, you could include a rock garden alongside the pond, or build a retaining stone wall instead. Unexciting shady areas may benefit from water features, although roots can make digging difficult and some trees lose their leaves in autumn.

Planters are like small gardens on their own and may be built in any number of locations – under a window, as part of a boundary wall, against a patio wall, or even in the center of a driveway or in the garden itself.

PRACTICAL DECORATION

While fences are generally made to enclose a property, they may also be built within the garden itself. Decorative picket fences can enclose a vegetable and herb garden, but may also be erected along a boundary – although be absolutely sure you know where the official boundary of your property lies. You may also need to get consent from your neighbours, who may automatically share ownership of the fence (or wall) even if they do not contribute towards the cost of it.

A rustic screen may make a patio more private or shield an entertainment area from prevailing winds. Before you start digging foundations, check whether there are any legal restrictions in terms of the height of the wall and its location. One can usually build small brick structures within the garden without approval, but walls and pillars to support a pergola roof, for example, may require plans. If you do need approval from your local authority, make sure that you do this before you rush out to buy materials.

STONE

OF ALL THE materials available for garden construction, stone is probably the most imposing. But it is also the most beautiful. A feature of the landscape forever, stone is the material that was used to build the earliest houses and fortress walls. Its very nature makes it highly durable but, ironically, it is not always easy to find and its weight often makes it difficult to work with.

Today, where stone is plentiful, houses and garden walls are still built from natural stone. In areas where it is not found naturally, anyone wishing to build with stone or incorporate rock gardens and stone features in their gardens will have to source it and transport it to the site. These logistical problems can make it an expensive material with which to build. However, people's love of stone all over the world has made it a rich and valuable inspiration for many constructions, and today many simulated stone materials are available. These range from fake flagstones to building units molded to look like natural stone wall capping. If you are unable to source natural stone, or if the costs place it beyond your reach, consider building features from precast concrete stone or paving with look-alike man-made slabs. Where rocks appear naturally in the garden, incorporate these into the garden plan, even if there is not sufficient material with which to actually build.

The projects that follow suggest various ways of using natural stone, from simply placing a selection of characteristic rocks and stone imaginatively to create a distinctly Oriental and wonderfully tranquil sand-and-stone garden to building dry wall structures using dressed stone and creating a path using broken slate and mortar. Various simulated slabs have also been utilized, both loosely laid and set in mortar. There are even instructions on how to make your own 'stone'. Most projects may be altered to use the real material in place of man-made alternatives, or precast concrete stone where the genuine article is not readily available.

IDEAS & INSPIRATION

When it comes to working with stone, nature herself is one of the greatest inspirations: from rocky outcrops and natural rock gardens to dry stone river beds and gravel wastelands, and even single stones simply strewn across the landscape. Despite being split, cut and moved, stone often blends with nature as though the hand of man had little to do with its creation.

water, rocks, sand and stone. The easiest style to emulate is that of meditative Zen Buddhists who created sand-and-stone arrangements purely for visual appreciation. Their aim was to reproduce a natural landscape, so a group of rocks around the base of a mound suggests a mountain, while a winding stepping-stone path across open gravel highlights the difficult route through life.

European influences

Many of the oldest fountains were of stone, although marble was common in ancient Rome, where elaborate water features were commonplace. In medieval gardens, marble was also favored for fountains, which were sometimes the garden's only really decorative features. Granite was often the material of choice in the great Italian gardens of the Renaissance, and modern, small-scale fountains, many of which originated in Italy, have been copied by craftsmen who mold them from concrete to look like stone.

ABOVE *Symbolically placed rocks may be arranged in a neatly raked sand garden typically Oriental in style.*

Italian landscapers of the 18th century began to imitate natural rock formations in large gardens and crags, precipices and caverns became the rage. Today, these are often made of precast concrete stone sculpted to create a similar look.

The Victorian preoccupation with new plant material inspired the use of rockwork in England, where gardeners copied the natural environment of many of the plants they had discovered. These included alpine gardens, which were sometimes planted in stone basins. One of the first rock gardens to attract any attention was built in a glass house at the Chelsea Physic Garden during the 19th century and utilized stones from the Tower of London, lava rock from Iceland, flint and even a little chalk.

The East revisited

Oriental landscapers value the use of stone, and the use of rocks, carefully chosen for their shape and form, has been characteristic of Eastern gardens since ancient times. Modern Oriental-style gardens focus on natural elements, with gravel and pebbles and round river rocks.

The Japanese also make great use of gravel and round stones. Today they are credited with having perfected the art of landscape gardening, with delicate arrangements of

Recreating the natural look

Many of the world's top landscapers believe that every stone in the garden should look as though it occurs there naturally, and most advise that today's gardeners should choose stone that occurs naturally in their area. At the same time, imaginative planning and a convincing layout can ensure 'imported' stone does not look out of place.

Unless you are prepared to pay to transport stone and rocks, you may be limited by what is readily available, but most garden features may now be built from precast concrete stone. This simulated product is lighter and easier to work with, and is also more accessible.

Generally, any structure that can be made with brick can also be built from stone, although the effect of natural rock will be quite different. Walls may be built with rocks or dressed stone, which is cut and patiently crafted; smaller features should generally be built using dressed stone, although it does not have to be perfectly cut.

Rock gardens built into sloping ground and 'natural' outcrops imitate nature. The secret is to make them look natural – as though the rocks have been there forever.

ABOVE *An attractive rock garden constructed alongside a swimming pool looks best left in its natural state.*
BELOW *The established plant life around this retaining rock wall lends a country feel to an expansive garden.*

TOOLS, TIPS & TECHNIQUES

Working with stone is probably more challenging than working with any other building material in the garden. Not only is this material heavy and cumbersome, it also takes considerable effort to split into workable units. Since it is a product of nature, it may also be difficult to source. Happily, in recent years, more and more companies have managed to create precast concrete stone units in imitation of natural stone, enabling us to build authentic structures in our gardens and to pave garden floors with materials that mimic the real thing.

TOOLS

In truth, the traditional stonemason's toolkit is unlikely to resemble the collection of tools most DIY enthusiasts will utilize for garden stonework. But this does not mean that you cannot work with stone or include it in your garden plan. On the contrary, stone offers a vehicle no other material can offer. Like all well-established crafts, stonework has a mystique about it. Perhaps it is the natural beauty of the material, but it is more likely to be because it is seldom available commercially and techniques are not readily shared.

Basic items

You will need equipment to excavate soil for foundations or to accommodate rocks in a slope, but chances are that you already have these tools. A **spade** will be the most essential tool because, apart from digging with it, it can also be used to mix concrete for foundations or mortar for building – although a **shovel** is easier to work with when mixing concrete. When preparing a site for any sort of building work, a **garden fork**, as well as **rakes**, are also useful, although not essential. A **pick** can be invaluable if you need to excavate rocky or hard ground. A **tamper** or long-handled **sledgehammer** will be needed to compact hardpan and earth, but you can also use the end of a pole.

A good-quality **wheelbarrow**, with a pneumatic tire, is always handy, but if you are planning relatively extensive rockwork, a **sack barrow** or trolley of some sort will probably be worth the additional investment. These have a flat surface, which is closer to the ground, making it easier to heave rocks around. A sack barrow is also levered, so you can move heavier weights on your own without the risk of injury. A **crowbar** is useful when shifting stone, although it is not much help if you have to move it a great distance.

Rake   Spade   Shovel   Fork

String & pegs   Wheelbarrow

Sack barrow

For laying out walls and other structures, use a ball of **string** and homemade **pegs** to demarcate boundaries and mark out straight lines. Alternatively, invest in metal pegs and builder's line. Smaller projects can be laid out using a little **lime**, **chalk** or even a small quantity of flour from the kitchen.

Even the smallest structures must be laid out accurately, so a good-quality retractable **metal tape measure** is indispensable. You will also use this to check the height of structures, as well as the dimensions of cut stone. When it comes to throwing concrete foundations, you will need a straight-edged length of wood to compact the mixture.

Stonework

Stone can be hard on the hands, so **protective gloves** are good for lifting and cutting. **Goggles** will protect your eyes from chips and dust when cutting stone or sawing with an angle grinder. Ideally, you should also wear a **dust mask**.

The most difficult aspect of stonework is breaking and cutting the stone. Even though ready-cut stone may be available (at greater cost), you will need **chisels** and a **stonemason's hammer**. The broad blade of a **brick chisel** is ideal for chopping or breaking rocks, but a **cold chisel**,

which has a smaller blade, may also be used. A **brick hammer** (which has a chisel at one end) is useful for breaking pieces off rock, but does not offer the accuracy of a chisel. Also be prepared to 'dress' the stone, which means chipping away until the face that will be exposed is reasonably flat.

A true stonemason will have a range of cutting tools, including chisels and a point (or punch), which has a pointed tip to concentrate the force of the hammer on one place. The most versatile carving tool is a **scutch holder** which, unlike a one-piece chisel, has a replaceable, double-edged (and sometimes toothed) cutting edge. If stone is to be cut at an angle, the professional will also use an adjustable, **two-armed bevel**.

An **electric angle grinder** cuts flagstones and simulated stone. Work on a flat, stable surface, and preferably outside, as you will generate a huge amount of dust.

Bricklaying tools are also useful. A **carpenter's level** ensures structures are level, and you will need a **trowel** to apply mortar. A **rubber mallet** is a necessity if laying flagstone or precast concrete pavers. This tool may also be used to tap stone into place when building walls and other structures as it will not chip the stone even if used with great force.

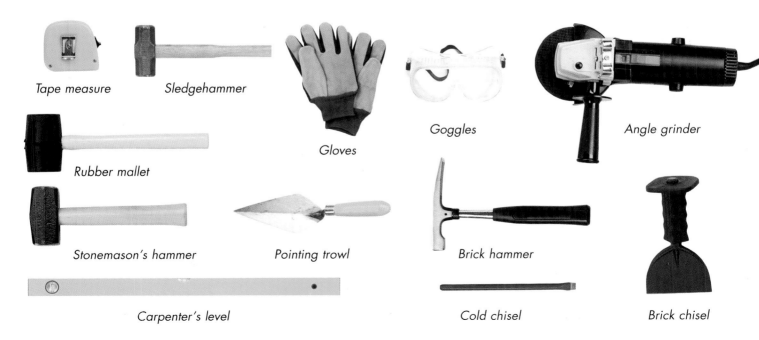

Tape measure   Sledgehammer

Rubber mallet

Gloves

Goggles

Angle grinder

Stonemason's hammer   Pointing trowl

Brick hammer

Carpenter's level

Cold chisel

Brick chisel

MATERIALS & METHODS

Limestone, sandstone and slate are the most universal natural stone types utilized in gardens all over the world. Granite may also be available, but it is very heavy and has a reputation as the graveyard stone. Precast concrete stone is widely available in a variety of forms for both building and paving, although ranges (including colors, sizes and shapes) depend on local manufacturers.

Stone

Quarried from the earth, natural stone comes in many guises, depending on the way it was formed. It may be split and dressed or cut, or used as it is found in nature.

■ **Granite** has been used for both building and ornamental purposes for centuries. Traditional setts (or cut cobbles) for walkways and pavements were made from granite. Unpolished granite was also a common material for curbstones, which may still be salvaged from road-works or demolition yards. Like the raw rock, which is exceedingly dense in composition, curbstones are very heavy and it takes several people to shift just one stone. Smaller granite rocks may be available from quarries. Granite also makes a good table top or kitchen counter and, because of its beauty, is popular as a headstone.

■ **Sandstone**, used for several of the projects featured here, is colored by small quantities of minerals, and may be gray, yellow, brown, red, or a combination of sandy hues. Usually relatively soft and easy to work with, it is ideal for rock gardens and both mortared and dry-stone walls. Properly cut, it may also be used for stepping stones or as larger flagstones. Since it forms in layers underground, some sandstone tends to split and flake.

■ **Limestone**, which – like sandstone – is formed in layers, was traditionally used to create enormous flagstones for flooring and for steps, as well as blocks for building. Like granite, it has become expensive, and most people prefer the reconstituted option, which looks remarkably like the real thing – either a dull gray or pinkish color.

■ **Slate** is usually split into thin sheets and used for roofing, floor tiles or, if broken, for cleft stone paving (*see pages 44–47*). Fine-grained, it is most commonly dark gray, but may also be dark green or a bluish-purple color.

■ **Flint** is an extremely hard form of silica often found in chalk foundations, and is sometimes split to produce one flat face for use as cobbles. Although not very common, flint is occasionally used with pebbles for walls. For stability, bricks are often used as a foundation, as well as at corners and as a capping.

Polished granite

Cobblestone

Round river stones

Sandstone

Small stone chips

■ Natural **cobblestones**, which may sometimes be found in fields, along river beds or on beaches, may be used to pave pathways and patios. Before you remove cobblestones – or any rock or stone – make sure that you are not on private property or that local by-laws do not prohibit the removal of indigenous rock and stone.

Precast concrete stone

Made in molds from crushed stone that has been mixed with cement, which is often colored to look like real rocks, precast concrete stone blocks and slabs have improved tremendously over the last few decades. Some innovative manufacturers have increased their product lines, not only creating molds from a growing number of local rock types, but also introducing a greater range of natural colors and types – particularly a range of slabs that may be used for paving. Some of the more innovative wall blocks include those that have a face molded to look like several randomly shaped stones, as well as modules that form a convincing coping, which looks as if individual stones have been placed on edge. Some of the single units have particularly realistically textured faces and, together with jumper blocks (which span two or more courses), can be used to create walls that look as though they have been built with natural dressed stone.

Ordinary gray concrete blocks, bricks and slabs bear no resemblance to stone and should generally be avoided unless they are to be rendered or, in the case of slabs, used out of sight.

Aggregate

Used as the coarse aggregate in concrete, ordinary crushed stone is generally available in several graded sizes, including ¾in (19mm) and ½in (13mm). Gravel, which is also crushed and graded, is generally an even finer material. Some crushed stones and gravels may be used for paths and patios, either on their own or combined with other materials.

Fine gravel looks particularly attractive if it is spread between irregularly shaped precast stone paving slabs. The color of the crushed material obviously depends on the color of the original stone, but brownish colors are generally the most attractive for this purpose.

Stone chips and round pebbles of various sizes are sometimes sold through garden shops and nurseries. Not practical for patios, it can be used in open beds or for sand or stone garden features.

The other aggregate used for stonework is, of course, sand. Standard 'sharp' building sand is generally used for concretework, while a much softer sand is required for mixing mortar, to which lime may also be added to make the mixture more cohesive. Coarse sand may also be used for bed-paving units.

ABOVE *A garden wall built from precast concrete stone blocks matches the material used to build the house.*

WALLS

When building walls with stone, the effect is generally much more random than when building with brick, particularly when building rubble walls, which utilize uncut or rough-cut stone and mortar. Since the shape of the stones used for rubble walls is irregular, the stone courses are not regular either. To add stability to the structure, include a relatively flat course (if you can) every 12in (300mm) or so. Cheaper to build than dressed stone walls, rubble walls are just as time-consuming to actually construct as they are a little like a three-dimensional jigsaw puzzle – and you will have to find the right size and shape of stone to fill the gap. In fact, there is little doubt that one of the greatest skills of a successful stonemason is his ability to select the correct stones.

Unlike rubble walls, freestanding dry-stone walls are usually quite thick and taper towards the top. More at home in the country than in the city, they have been a feature of the landscape of many countries for centuries. Since they take a large quantity of stone to construct, they are only an option in areas where stone is plentiful and, preferably, free. These walls are laid on a well-compacted sand base, with a foundation of large, flat stones. Before you start laying the wall itself, you will need to make two batter boards from four lengths of timber nailed together to form an easel shape, with pointed ends on the wider underside. These points are pushed into the soil at either end of the wall and used in place of a bricklayer's cornerblock, to hold a string line that will enable you to keep to the correct shape of the wall.

ABOVE *A rubble wall constructed to retain soil alongside a pool is the perfect foil for a tropical garden.*

ABOVE *A retaining stone wall built with mortar helps support a rock garden on the slope above.*

Large, square or rectangular stones are often used at ends and corners (hence the term 'cornerstone'). Although the central cavity is usually filled with broken stones, every now and then, a long tie stone should be laid across the wall to create a natural bond and ensure that the structure is stable and well balanced. If you want to plant a dry-stone wall, it may be easier to fill the central cavity with earth instead.

Although a retaining stone wall is similar in structure to a freestanding dry-stone wall, it slopes backwards in one direction instead of sloping inwards from the foundation on both sides. The height of the wall will determine the type of foundations required. Low walls may need no foundation other than well-compacted earth, but if it is to restrain a great volume of earth, compacted stone and

ABOVE *Stone boulders have been cleverly incorporated in an unusual, architect-designed garden wall.*

concrete should be included in the design. Mix the concrete 1:4:4 with sand and crushed stone and combine with sufficient water to make the mixture easily workable but not too wet. If the wall is to be any higher than 5ft (1.5m), you will also need to allow for drainage or it could collapse. Alternatively, slope the wall at a very gentle angle. If in doubt, consult an engineer for advice.

While rock gardens may be similar to stone retaining walls in some ways, they are really only suitable for gentle slopes.

If using mortar to build a stone wall, use a general 1:6 cement:sand mix, adding half as much lime as cement to the mixture.

RETAINING ROCK GARDEN

CREATED TO RETAIN the soil on a slope in the corner of a country garden, this 6½ft-wide (2m) sandstone rock garden not only adds interest between two grassy terraces, it also has a practical function. Plants indigenous to the area have been set in deep pockets of soil between the rocks, offering a contrast of both color and texture. Once established, the root systems of the various plants will also help bind the soil.

1 DAY

YOU WILL NEED

TOOLS
- wheelbarrow
- shovel and/or spade
- pegs and stonemason's hammer
- carpenter's level
- straight-edged length of wood (optional)
- builder's gloves (optional)

MATERIALS
- rocks: 20 large rocks (maximum 20in/ 500mm dimension); about 20 smaller rocks (4–8in/100–200mm)
- soil (may be required for fill or planting pockets, depending on the site)

RECREATING NATURE

A rock garden is easily created on virtually any slope, provided it is not too high or too steep, in which case a retaining wall with proper drainage is usually a more sensible option. Here, the top terrace is only 4ft (1.2m) above the groundline, even though at the spot chosen for the rock garden previous excavations had not allowed the ground to slope at all. By digging into the bank a gentle incline is formed and the excess soil is utilized to backfill and thus hold the rocks in place, as well as to form deep pockets of earth where plants can establish themselves.

The sandstone rocks were from a nearby building excavation, but the principles illustrated may be adapted to whatever rocks and stones you have on site or are able to source. No special tools are necessary for this project; all you need is a wheelbarrow and spade – and lots of muscle and determination.

TIP When planting a rock garden, use a small spade to check the depth of the earth pocket. Inevitably, a few of these will be formed on top of other rocks; in this instance, choose plants that do not need much space to develop a root system in order to anchor themselves. If planting cacti or succulents, remove some of the soil from the earth pockets and replace with crushed stone or gravel for added drainage.

1 Decide on the position of the retaining rock garden and peg out an area at least 6½ft (2m) wide, 23½in (600mm) from the bottom of the existing bank.

2 Remove grass and any other vegetation to create a relatively flat foundation for the base rocks. Dig away excess soil and keep to one side for use later.

3 Use a straight-edged piece of wood and/or a carpenter's level to ensure that your foundation is flat and level. Be sure to compact the earth thoroughly.

4 Use a wheelbarrow to move the rocks close to the site. Position large, flattish rocks at the front of the 'foundation' on which other rocks can balance.

5 Place a row of rocks along the front, filling any gaps between the large rocks with smaller rocks. Some of these rocks will inevitably be covered with soil; even though they will not be visible, they are, however, vital in preventing the soil from eroding or seeping out of the pockets created for planting.

6 Dig into the bank to create a gentle slope. Backfill behind the first row of rocks until the upper soil level is no more than 4in (100mm) below the largest rocks. Compact the soil before placing a second layer of rocks behind the first. When placing these, be sure to leave sufficient space between the rocks to create deep earth pockets.

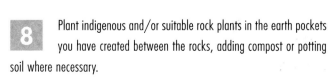

7 Continue working your way systematically up the slope, using large rocks at either end of the rock garden to retain the soil. Wedge each rock into position and backfill with soil.

8 Plant indigenous and/or suitable rock plants in the earth pockets you have created between the rocks, adding compost or potting soil where necessary.

STONE STEPS

NATURAL STONE STEPS not only create a link between two distinct garden areas and provide a safe, dry route from one level of the garden to the other, they also add charm and character and invite one to explore further. Perfect for the informal layout of this garden, the irregular design curves slightly and looks as though it was placed there, quite simply, by nature.

1 DAY

YOU WILL NEED

TOOLS

- shovel and/or spade
- builder's gloves
- tape measure
- carpenter's level
- brick and chisel hammer
- stonemason's hammer
- brick or broad chisel

MATERIALS

- rocks: 12 large but reasonably flat-topped rocks; 6–12 smaller stones
- stone chips or gravel: 300lbs/135kg

A STEP ABOVE THE REST

The construction of stone steps in the garden will depend on several factors, including the degree of the slope and the size and shape of rocks available, as well as the soil on which they are to be built. Creating steps on a gentle slope like this one is a relatively simple task. No special stonework tools are necessary, although you may need a brick or broad chisel to chip away uneven edges. While formal stone steps built up a steep incline will invariably require a concrete foundation and, more often than not, mortar to keep them in place, flat-topped rocks may be set into a stable slope to create an informal arrangement without concrete or mortar. Some form of drainage will be needed behind most steps, unless, like these, they are very gradual and are sited away from existing buildings.

Because the rocks will inevitably be rather heavy, start the operation by moving a selection of suitable rocks and smaller stones to the site. Then remove all the existing vegetation from the slope where the steps are to be built.

Materials detailed here will make six steps.

TIP If a rock is uneven and moves when walked on, place smaller stones and soil underneath it to help stabilize it. Also use additional smaller stones wherever there is a possibility of rain washing away the soil and eroding the structure.

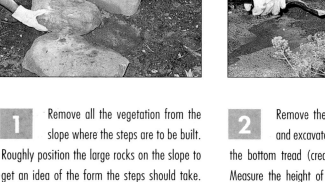

1 Remove all the vegetation from the slope where the steps are to be built. Roughly position the large rocks on the slope to get an idea of the form the steps should take. (Don't worry about the upper level of the rocks: you will need to excavate the soil before placing them permanently.)

2 Remove the first two or three rocks and excavate an area to accommodate the bottom tread (created by two rocks here). Measure the height of the rocks and dig away this depth, plus 2in (50mm) to accommodate a foundation. Ensure that the base slopes slightly away from the bank to assist drainage.

3 Pour a 2in (50mm) layer of stone chips into the trench you have dug, spreading the stones evenly along the bottom of the trench. This will not only help you level the rocks you place on top, but will also help to facilitate drainage of the area once the steps have been built.

4 Wiggle the first rock into position into the gravel and use the chisel end of the hammer to 'chop' the stones in under the rock to stabilize it. Then use the top end of the club hammer to wedge the chips under gaps and into the softer ground. Place the second rock in position, compacting and chipping the gravel under it as before.

5 The tread of each step should slope away from the bank to aid drainage. Use a carpenter's level to check that you have achieved a slight slope. You can also use the carpenter's level as a straight edge to check that the surface is sufficiently flat to walk on. If it isn't, you may have to chip away rough bumps, or use a different shaped rock.

6 Fill in around the first two rocks with more of the gravel and then, if necessary, use smaller stones to complete the tread. Wedge chips under the rocks to make the tread more stable. Remember that you do not want the chips to be visible once the steps are complete and these should eventually be covered by soil.

7 Cover and fill any gaps with gravel; chop in with the two hammers and cover with a thin layer of soil.

8 Excavate the soil to create a base for two more rocks, 2in (50mm) below the surface of the first tread.

9 Pour stone into the trench and position a rock. If the rock is unstable, cut the uneven edge with a broad chisel and hammer.

10 Reposition the first rock on the gravel so that it rests on the edge of the first tread. Position the second rock of the second tread in exactly the same way, wiggling it into the gravel as before.

11 Position smaller stones within or next to this tread and fill the gaps with gravel as described in Step 4. Ensure the tread is even and slopes very slightly from the back.

12 Continue creating treads until you reach the top of the slope. Plant on either side of the steps. If you have additional rocks and stones, you could also create a rock garden or rock garden on each side of the steps, planting in pockets between the rocks.

SERENE STONE GARDEN

EMULATING THE GARDEN philosophies of the Orient, particularly China and Japan, this remarkably tranquil little stone garden transforms what was once a bare patch under a pepper tree. While the statue of Buddha gives this patch a Chinese feel, a Japanese lantern or stone water basin would give it an equally Japanese touch.

1 WEEKEND

YOU WILL NEED

TOOLS
- wheelbarrow
- shovel and/or spade
- craft knife

MATERIALS
- rocks/stones: 4 large; 8 slightly smaller; 60 stones x 4–8in (100–200mm)
- stone chips/gravel: 53–70 cubic ft (1.5–2m³)
- black polyethylene: 16½ft x 16½ft (5m x 5m) x 500 micron (to cover 12 sq yd/10m²)
- plastic edging strip: 52½ft/16m
- paving stones: 9 stones x 20in x 20in (500mm x 500mm); 9 stones x 10in x 20in (250mm x 500mm)
- sand (optional): 30lbs/13.5kg
- features (optional): statue of Buddha; frog; Oriental pot, planter
- driftwood (optional)

AT PEACE WITH SAND AND STONE

The modern 'still' garden, currently popular in Europe, takes its cue from the ancient gardens of the East. In the Chinese garden, rocks and water are traditionally the principal elements, with contrasting features (rough and smooth, big and small) introducing the philosophy of yin and yang and its unique balance of nature. Sand and stone gardens are more typical of the Japanese temple garden, with sand and small round pebbles often representing the river of life.

The rocks and stones used to create this tranquil garden were all found on the property, although the intriguing variety indicates that at least some of them did not occur there naturally. The crushed stone (gravel chips) was purchased from a garden center. Use what you have or seek out what will work for your own area. You will need at least three or four large 'guardian' stones and several other smaller ones with texture and character. The statue and plants you choose will help create the look you desire. The stone slab pathway adds to the character, at the same time giving easy access to the plants.

> **TIP** A shallow layer of sand laid over the plastic will make it easier to level the stone slabs.

1 Roughly mark out a circle with a 16½ft (5m) diameter, and remove all grass and vegetation. If you want to incorporate a sprinkler system, install the pipework now, burying it underground with risers at several points.

2 Dig a shallow trench around the circumference of the circle. It need not be any deeper than 4in (100mm) unless you opt for an alternative edging that requires a foundation. Make sure that the surface of the 'garden' is flat and level.

3 Position the four large rocks and any features, you have chosen, including statues, to create the form and feel of the garden.

4 Cover the entire surface of the circle with black plastic, cutting around the rocks and cutting off the corners with a craft knife.

5 Position the rest of the rocks and stones, together with a selection of suitable plants. Three different conifers, a large fern, bamboo and Japanese Mondo grass create the effect beautifully.

6 Place the edging in the trench around the circumference of the circle, gradually filling the trench up with soil as you work. Cut holes in the plastic in order to accommodate the plants and dig holes into which you can sink them. By leaving them in the black bags in which many nurseries and garden centres grow their plants, you will limit their growth and thus maintain a bonsai effect. If you want to encourage growth, remove the bags prior to planting.

7 Lay the paving stones on the plastic or on a shallow layer of sand (about ¾in/20mm), alternating the two different sizes. Cover the plastic with stone chips. Plant grass around the edge of the 'garden' to create a contrast of color and texture.

STONE SLAB PATIO

WHETHER SLABS ARE made of simulated stone or from the real thing, they make a beautifully hard-wearing and attractive surface for any patio area. Four different slab sizes have been used here to create interest and to introduce a random pattern. Several areas within the courtyard have been left unpaved and topped with gravel, adding texture and providing a natural surface for groups of potted plants. Patio furniture gives the area its own distinctive style while at the same time providing a perfect place for alfresco eating and casual entertaining.

1–2 WEEKS

YOU WILL NEED

TOOLS

- shovel and/or spade
- tape measure
- tamper or compacting machine
- carpenter's level
- broom

MATERIALS

- slabs: 25 slabs x 26in x 17½in (660mm x 440mm); 25 slabs x 17½in x 17½in (440mm x 440mm); 25 slabs x 17½in x 8¾in (440mm x 220mm); 26 slabs x 8¾in x 8¾in (220mm x 220mm)
- sand: 21 cubic ft (0.6m³)

TIP If you decide to lay the entire bed of sand before laying the slabs, hose the sand layer down lightly to help it remain compact. Use slabs as stepping stones across the compacted sand.

THE PERFECT PATIO

Simulated stone slabs laid on a thick bed of sand form a patio that will blend well with any garden design, while plants and garden furniture chosen will set the style.

Four slab sizes are used for this project, and no particular pattern of laying has been specified. Sizes increase in 8¾in (220mm) units from the smallest (8¾in x 8¾in/220mm x 220mm) to a rectangular (8¾in x 17½in/220mm x 440mm) slab, a larger (17½in x 17½in/440mm x 440mm) square, and finally to the largest rectangular slab (17½in x 26in/440mm x 660mm) – while quantities specified will cover an area of 19 sq yd (16m²). Like genuine stone slabs, these precast concrete units vary slightly in thickness from about 1in (25mm) to 1½in (35mm). This means that the final surface may be slightly uneven, just as stone would be. Ask your supplier for sufficient slabs to cover the patio area you wish to pave.

If your patio is not contained within a courtyard, you will probably need an edging of either timber or stone. Cobbles could also be used (*see page 21*). These materials are not specified.

Slabs may also be laid on a concrete foundation with a narrow mortar joint between them. Alternatively, where the ground is not particularly stable, or where a patio is built into a slight slope, throw a foundation slab and top this with a thick 2in (50mm) sand bed before you begin laying the slabs.

1 If the patio is not enclosed, first peg out an area measuring 13ft x 13ft (4m x 4m). Remove grass and vegetation and level the area. The base of the patio must be stable, and some sites may require a well-compacted sub-base of crushed stone, which needs to be covered with soil before being compacted again. Presuming your site is already stable, compact the soil and use a long plank as a straight edge, with a carpenter's level on top of it, to check that the surface is level. Move the plank around the entire area, positioning it in different directions. It is easier to correct levels at this stage than having to remove slabs and dig away excess soil later.

2 Before spreading sand over the base, use a weed killer — mixed with water according to the manufacturer's instructions — over the entire surface. This will prevent unwanted grass and unsightly weeds from springing up through the slabs at a later stage.

3 Spread a 1–2in (25–50mm) layer of sand over the section of the patio where you want to start paving. Draw the plank towards you to flatten and smooth out the sand. Remember that the final surface should slope slightly to aid drainage. This is particularly important if it is next to the house or any other building, in which case the surface should slope away from the structure.

4 Start laying the slabs in the center of the patio, at one end, and work out from adjacent walls. Butt each of the slabs right up against the one alongside it.

5 Use the carpenter's level to check that the slabs are level and slope slightly. If they are not, lift and either remove or add a little sand under the offending slab. If the slabs are not at all level, remove the uneven slabs and use the carpenter's level to flatten the sand surface.

6 Add more sand to the base as you need it and experiment with the different-sized pavers to create an attractive pattern. Change the pattern of the pavers if you are not happy with it. The most important factor is to keep the pavers level.

7 Keep checking the horizontal planes of the ground with a long carpenter's level as you work.

8 Once all the slabs are in place, brush sand over the entire surface to fill any gaps that remain between the slabs.

PATTERNED PATHWAY

A MAGICAL MOSAIC of precast concrete stone pavers and cobbles, as well as natural river stones, colored tiles and even the odd polished stones creates unusual texture and adds color and interest to a small herb and vegetable garden. Ideal for any style of garden, this particular path is irregular and informal, but could easily be adapted to incorporate a more geometric design.

YOU WILL NEED

TOOLS

- shovel and/or spade
- builder's line or string
- tape measure
- chalk, hydrated lime or flour
- pole or tamper
- carpenter's level
- trowel
- rubber mallet

MATERIALS

- flagstones/precast concrete stone pavers: 5 pavers x 30in x 20in x 2⅓in (750mm x 500mm x 60mm); 6 pavers x 10in x 10in x 2½in (250mm x 250mm x 60mm)
- precast concrete stone edging blocks: 24 blocks x 12in x 3⅓in x 4in (300mm x 85mm x 100mm); 24 blocks x ¾in x 3⅓in x 4in (200mm x 85mm x 100mm)
- precast concrete stone cobbles/pavers: 79 pavers x 4⅓in x 4⅓in x 2⅓in (110mm x 110mm x 60mm)
- river stones: 151 (various sizes and colors)
- crushed stone: 221–1158lbs (100–525kg)
- sand: 221–584lbs (100–265kg)
- mortar: 110lbs (50kg) cement; 441lbs (200kg); sand

3–4 DAYS

STYLED IN STONE

Laid on sand with paving units partially embedded in mortar, this unusual garden path combines a variety of elements that may easily be mixed and matched to accommodate your own particular garden design and style. Large 30in x 20in (750mm x 500mm) precast concrete stone paving slabs similar to flagstones determine the width of the path (30in/750mm). These units also form a solid tread between ingenious designs made with a combination of precast cobbles (pavers), slabs and smaller pavers to which natural stones have been added. A precast concrete stone edging holds the path together and, at the same time, unifies the design. When choosing materials for your path, try to maintain some uniformity when it comes to the height of flagstones and pavers. If these are not the same height, you will need extra mortar to bolster the height of the smaller units.

Materials specified here will allow you to build a 16½ft-long (6m) path with four patterned sections, 30in x 25½–35½in (750mm x 650–900mm) in size.

> **TIP** A completely different effect may be achieved by using a combination of different sized and colored bricks.

1 Decide where you want to lay a path. Lay one flagstone at each end of the path and use this as a guide to its width. String a line between the two pavers and mark with chalk, hydrated lime or flour. Repeat on the other side of the path.

2 Excavate a trench between the two lines of up to 8in (200mm) deep, depending on the condition of your soil.

3 Fill the trench with between ¾in (20mm) and 4in (100mm) of crushed stone and compact with the end of a heavy pole or with a tamper to create a hardcore base.

4 Top the hardcore with ¾–2in (20–50mm) of sand and use a long carpenter's level as a straight edge to smooth and level.

5 Lay the first flagstone on the sand at one end. String a new line 3⅓in (85mm) from the edge of the stone to allow for the edging. Loosely lay a few of the edging stones.

6 Loosely lay the pavers on the sand along the full length of the path, positioning pavers, smaller pavers and stones to create the desired patterns. Use a capenter's level to ensure that the pavers are all level.

7 When you are reasonably happy with the design of the path, mix mortar and lay the edging stones on either side of the path. Knock down firmly with a rubber mallet.

8 Once it is cemented in place, the edging will make it easier for you to create the pattern features between the larger pavers. Where river stones, tiles and the like are to be used, fill the area with mortar and use a trowel to compact, level and smooth it out. Work systematically, and only tackle one section at a time.

9 Now push the stones into the wet mortar with the flattest side uppermost. If using tiles, scrape a little mortar from the center of each block of mortar and position, gently pressing into the wet mix. If you don't like the pattern you have created, now is the time to change it.

10 Use the mallet to gently knock the stones and tiles deeper into the mortar. They should protrude slightly, but not enough to make the path hazardous or uncomfortable to walk on.

11 Fill the gaps between the pavers with mortar. Use a chopping movement with the trowel to ensure you fill the joints properly. Use a wet sponge to smooth the upper surface of wet mortar and clean the pavers at the same time.

12 Where flagstones are laid next to one another, leave gaps of between 2⅜in (60mm) and 5½in (140mm) and plant with creeping herbs or groundcover plants instead of filling with mortar. This will add even more color and texture to the path.

CLEFT STONE PAVING PATHWAY

BROKEN PIECES OF charcoal slate tile have been laid to create an inexpensive cleft stone paving path about 9ft (3m) long. An edging of rustic paving bricks in a contrasting color adds texture and another hue to the final picture. Used to link two areas within the garden, the 31½in-wide (800mm) curved pathway may also be constructed in a straight line from broken concrete slabs or stone pavers.

YOU WILL NEED

TOOLS

- shovel and/or spade
- chalk, hydrated lime or flour measure
- tape measure
- carpenter's level
- straight-edged piece of wood
- broom

MATERIALS

- slate/stone/tiles: broken material to cover 2½ sq yds (2m²)
- bricks: 25
- sand: 55lbs (25kg)
- grout: 44lbs (20kg) cement; 44lbs (20kg) sand

1 WEEKEND

FOOTPATH FUN

Incredibly popular as a low-cost solution to paved pathways and patios, cleft stone paving can be created from various broken and leftover materials, including slate, stone and tiles. The thickness of the material will determine, to a large extent, whether it can be laid on sand and grouted with a dry mortar mix or should rather be embedded in a cement-sand slush or mortar to aid cohesion.

Since this option is a rather practical one, attention should be given to peripheral planting to ensure that it contributes aesthetically to the surrounding area.

Materials specified here are for a curved pathway about 9ft (2.7m) long and 31½ft (800mm) wide. These dimensions and materials are easily adapted to any site.

TIPS If the material you are using is not very thick, then lay it on a cement-sand slush rather than directly on sand.

Use a combination of materials to introduce different colors. If the different tiles vary in thickness, lay on sand and add more under the thinner units.

1 Loosely lay the brick edging along either side of the outside edges of the planned pathway, which will be 31½in (800mm) wide. Mark the line of the bricks with chalk or hydrated lime.

2 Dig a trench just deep enough to accommodate the brick edging – in this case about 4in (100mm) deep. Position the edging, checking the 31½in (800mm) distance between the two sides as you work.

3 Remove the excess soil and any stones from the pathway itself and level the ground so that it is 1–1¼in (25–30mm) from the upper surface of the bricks.

4 Add a 1in (25mm) layer of sand over the excavated pathway and use a straight-edged piece of timber and/or a long carpenter's level to ensure that it is level.

5 Place the broken material on the sand bed, checking levels regularly. Producing an attractive pattern is a bit like producing a jigsaw from offcuts!

6 Once you have placed all the pieces of the 'puzzle', use a carpenter's level to check that all are flat and level. There should be a slight runoff for rain water.

7 Combine a strong, dry mix of sand and cement in the ratio 1:1. Brush this over the entire surface to fill all gaps. Gently spray water over the entire area, then allow to dry.

DECORATIVE STONE SEAT

DESIGNED AS AN outdoor seat, this small but decorative dry-stone structure could also be constructed to house a letterbox or act as a base for various other decorative features. The building method may be used for any seat or wall-like structure that is to be built from stone — from seating and table arrangements to screen walls devised to contain smaller areas within a garden.

1 WEEK

YOU WILL NEED

TOOLS

- wheelbarrow
- shovel and/or spade
- steel tape measure
- trowel
- chisels and a stonemason's hammer
- carpenter's level
- straight-edged length of wood (optional)
- builder's gloves (optional)

MATERIALS

- stone blocks: 3⅓ cubic yd (2.8m²) cut stone, 2–4in (50–100mm) thick
- stone chips/offcuts: 550lbs (250kg)
- concrete: 165lbs (75kg) cement; 660lbs (300kg) crushed stone; 660lbs (300kg) sand
- mortar: 220lbs (100kg) cement; 900lbs (400kg) sand; 110lbs (50kg) hydrated lime (optional)

SEAT OF STONE

The method of building dry-stone bases such as this has changed little over the centuries. Soil has always been used to help bind permanent structures and, before the manufacture of cement, local clay was used in much the same way as mortar is used today. If freestanding dry-stone structures are to be built without binding material (clay or mortar), it should be thicker at the base than at the top; for instance, a 6½ft-high (2m) seat should be about 23½in (600mm) thick at the base, tapering to about 17¾in (450mm).

Materials listed here are sufficient to build either a garden seat 3½ft (1m) long, 20in (500mm) thick and 27½in (700mm) high or a base for an outdoor lamp. About 25 neatly split and 'dressed' stone blocks are required; these may range in size from 10in x 8in (250mm x 200mm) to smaller 6in x 6in (150mm x 150mm) and 5½in x 4in (140mm x 100mm) blocks. If purchasing cut (or split) stone, ensure you have sufficient waste to fill the center of the seat; if ordering uncut stone, increase the quantity specified by 30–50 percent to allow for wastage when splitting and 'dressing'. Limestone may be an alternative to the sandstone used here.

TIP Cut the stone into blocks before you start and sort into units more or less the same size. Chip rough edges to make them fit as you work.

1 The foundation slab should be 4in (100mm) wider than the seat on all sides. Use pegs and line or string to mark out a boundary. The foundation area, marked out in chalk or hydrated lime, measures 4½ft x 35½in (1.4m x 900mm), allowing for an extra 8in (200mm) on each side.

2 Dig the foundation trench to a depth of 6in (150mm). Use a carpenter's level to check that the base of the trench is flat and level.

3 Mix the concrete and place into the trench. Flatten the concrete with the back of a shovel.

4 Use a straight-edged length of wood or a long carpenter's level to compact the concrete and rid it of air bubbles. Allow the concrete to set thoroughly for several hours, preferably overnight.

5 Choose stones of different sizes and lay two or three together on the dry concrete, pushing them against one another to ensure that they are flush and form a straight face. You may have to use a chisel and a stonemason's hammer to cut and chip away at the stone until it fits perfectly.

6 Once you are happy with the way the first few stones fit together, mix a small quantity of mortar and use a trowel to place it against the side of the stones that will face the seat cavity. This will help support the stone.

7 Continue working your way around the perimeter of the seat. After you have placed two or three stones, place more mortar on the inside face, pushing it into any crevices and gaps from the inside. Be careful not to allow the mortar to seep through to the outer face.

8 Once you have laid the first course of stones, carefully add broken stone and chips to the central cavity.

9 Place more of the mortar in-between the hardcore to form a solid concrete core.

10 Once the broken stone and mortar reaches the top of the smallest stone laid in the first course (layer), start the second course. Work in exactly the same way, placing the mortar on the stones' inside face and not between the courses.

11 Once the seat is complete, allow the mortar to set before laying flat coping stones along the top.

12 If the coping does not sit flush against the top of the seat, push stone chips into the gaps. Not only will this level the coping stones, but will also add to the appeal of the structure.

FORMAL GARDEN TABLE

CAREFULLY CUT STONE is a remarkably effective material for building a garden table suitable for entertaining. Stone slabs of various sizes have been used to create the effect of dry-stone walls supporting a wonderfully natural, solid sandstone table top. It is built under an established tree, which offers shade from the sun, while its foliage adds to the ambience of the outdoor area. This design would be equally effective on a stone slab patio or in a courtyard paved with flagstones or precast concrete slabs.

2 WEEKENDS

YOU WILL NEED

TOOLS

- wheelbarrow
- shovel and/or spade
- steel tape measure
- chisels and a stonemason's hammer
- carpenter's level
- trowel
- straight-edged length of wood (optional)
- builder's gloves (optional)

MATERIALS

- stone blocks: 2 sq yrds (1.5m²) cut stone, 2–4in (50–100mm) thick
- stone chips/offcuts: 220lbs (100kg) of varying sizes
- stone slab: 40in x 34in x 2in (1m x 850 mm x 50 mm) sandstone
- concrete: 66lbs (30kg) cement; 265lbs (120kg) crushed stone; 265lbs (120kg) sand
- mortar: 110lbs (50kg) cement; 440lbs (200kg) sand; 55lbs (25kg) lime (optional)

DINING IN STYLE

The most difficult part of this project will probably be finding a suitable slab of stone to top the table. The only other really tricky task will involve transporting this slab and lifting it onto the two supporting piers, so make sure you have able and willing help.

The stone chosen for the project will depend on what is available in your area. If cut stone is not available, you may have to split and 'dress' it yourself – in which case it is essential to choose stone that is soft enough to break, cut and chip without necessarily having to resort to expensive specialist tools. Sandstone, supplied in reasonably regular blocks, was used for this project, but limestone blocks may also be suitable. The alternative is to opt for precast concrete stone blocks, which are regular in shape and relatively easy to cut.

Materials specified here are a guide only. When buying stone for the project, remember that if you are going to cut your own blocks to shape, you will need to start with considerably more stone than you will need to use as there will inevitably be wastage. The offcuts and chips may, however, be used in the pier (support) cavities.

Constructing the two piers for the table is like piecing together a three-dimensional jigsaw puzzle. Although mortar is used, the blocks are not bedded in it; instead, the inner cavity is filled with broken stone and the mortar mixture so that the inner surface of the walls bind with it – on the inside only. The secret is to ensure that the stonework bonds, block on block, as building progresses. If one stone is out of alignment, it will affect the entire structure.

1 The size of the piers (supports) will be determined by the size of your table top. If yours is not the same size as that specified here, adjust the measurements of the two foundations to fit. If you can find a slab the same size, measure out two 31½in x 12in (800mm x 300mm) areas, 12in (300mm) apart. Mark their position using hydrated lime, cement or chalk. Alternatively, peg out the foundations using pegs and builder's line or string.

2 Dig two trenches to a depth of 4in (100mm). If building on a slight slope, dig deeper on the upper level so that the base of each foundation is on exactly the same plane. Place several bricks on top of one another in each trench and place a long carpenter's level across them to check that the base is indeed flat and level. Mix the concrete and then place in both the trenches. Use a straight edge or carpenter's level to compact the concrete and check that it is level. Allow it to set, preferably overnight.

3 If you are cutting your own stone, choose a flat, level site close to where you will be building. Transport the stone in a wheelbarrow, and then use chisels and a stonemason's hammer to split and chip them to shape. The slabs should be about 2⅜in (60mm) thick — no thinner than about 2in (50mm) and no thicker than 4in (100mm). Suitable sizes vary immensely, and they may be square or rectangular. It does not matter if thicknesses vary; in fact, this will add strength to the structure. Be sure that you have a good selection of cut-stone units before you mix the mortar and start building.

4 Experiment with a few blocks of stone, setting them freely on the foundation. When you are happy with the arrangement, mix a little of the mortar in a wheelbarrow or on a flat, dry surface. Make sure your first few stones are standing solidly together and place mortar in the central cavity that is starting to form. Push the mortar against the inner walls of the stone with the trowel, pushing gently into all crevices however small, but without moving the stone slabs apart.

5 Once the first row of stone slabs is securely in place, place chips and offcuts into the cavity with more of the mortar.

6 Working with varying sizes, continue laying the stone on edge, filling the cavity with mortar as you do so. If the slabs you have already cut do not fit snugly, remove and chip a little off one or more edges until they fit properly.

7 Edges will never be completely straight, so use chips under the blocks whenever necessary to level them. Keep checking with a carpenter's level to make certain that both horizontal and vertical surfaces are properly aligned. Also, be sure to keep topping up the mortar and stone offcuts in the central cavity as you work. If you leave the center hollow for any time, the walls are likely to collapse.

8 Build both piers up to a height of 27½in (700mm) and use the carpenter's level, with a straight edge if necessary, to ensure they are flat, level and properly aligned. Place a bed of about ½in (15mm) of mortar on top of each pier and use the level or a straight edged length of timber to scrape both sides flat. Again, check that both sides are level. Allow to set thoroughly before placing the slab on top.

HYPERTUFA SINK GARDEN

CONTAINER GARDENING IS popular all over the world and the size and styles of containers are as vast and varied as the plants that grow in them. A relatively recent craze was to plant alpine plants in stone or simulated stone sinks. In the absence of a genuine stone sink, keen gardeners in the first half of the 20th century developed a technique to cover old white glazed sinks with a 'hypertufa' mix to make them look like stone. More recently, troughs have been cast from hypertufa to create containers that resemble this fascinating volcanic tufa rock.

YOU WILL NEED

TOOLS

- chalk, hydrated lime or pegs and builder's line/string
- builder's square
- tape measure
- carpenter's level
- spade
- pole (to compact the hypertufa)

MATERIALS

- pegs: 2 pegs x 8in x ¾in (200mm x 20mm)
- hypertufa: 110lbs (50kg) cement; 110lbs (50kg) coarse sand; 220lbs (100kg) sphagnum peat or peat moss
- metal grid: 25½in x 18in (650mm x 450mm)
- potting soil
- suitable plants

2 WEEKENDS

CAST IN STONE

Original hypertufa sinks were made by painting chunky old white sinks with a PVA adhesive and, once this was tacky, coating the surface with a mixture of sphagnum peat, sand, cement and water. The results were quite remarkable and the popularity of growing alpine plants in these stone lookalike containers grew rapidly.

Some commercial manufacturers have now developed ways to simulate stone sink designs and a few enthusiasts have experimented with hypertufa mixtures, casting their own sinks in the ground. An original recipe for coating glazed sinks involved mixing 2 parts of peat with 1 part of sand and 1 part cement. The materials called for in this project are similar, but instead of coating an existing sink, the mixture is cast in a hole in the ground and dug out once it has thoroughly set. Coarse sand is used as this gives the finished item a stone-like texture.

TIPS Hypertufa and other simulated stone troughs can be very heavy. If you want to move yours, wrap rope around it and use a vehicle with a towbar to tow it slowly across the ground.

If there is any danger of rain while the sink is curing, cover it with plastic.

1 Find an area in the garden where you can dig without disturbing the established plants. Make sure that the earth is reasonably well compacted; soft soil collapses and you will not be able to dig a hole with straight walls that will be suitable as a mold. Measure a rectangle no larger than 33½in x 25½in (850mm x 650mm). Mark out with pegs or chalk and use a builder's square to check that the corners are square. Dig out ½–⅝in (12–15mm) of soil, being very careful to keep the walls absolutely straight. Now comes the tricky part: dig to a depth of 10in (250mm), but around the outside only. Use a steel tape to measure about ½in (12mm) in from each side and mark out a smaller rectangle using chalk or hydrated lime. As you continue to dig, you will need to ensure that all vertical walls remain straight. If the soil collapses or you dig at an angle, your mold will be ruined and you will have to start again. Once it is complete, carefully knock the two dowels into the raised soil about 1¼in (30mm) apart.

2 Mix the hypertufa in a wheelbarrow, in batches in precisely the same way as you would mix mortar, taking care not to add too much water to the mixture.

3 Carefully place the mixture into the outside trenches of the mold. Be careful not to damage the walls of the mold. Use a pole to compact the hypertufa around the outside to expel all the air bubbles. This will ensure the sides of the sink are strong and solid.

4 Add another ⅕in (5mm) of hypertufa over the entire surface before placing the wire grid over the two dowels protruding from what will be the bottom of the sink; then cover the mesh with more of the hypertufa mixture. Compact gently with a straight-edged piece of wood and allow to set thoroughly for about a week.

5 To remove the sink, carefully dig around the mold so that you gradually expose the outer walls. Once all the walls are exposed, use a couple of strong poles to ease the sink out of the ground. Scrape the soil from the center of the trough and rinse with water. Fill with potting soil and plant with alpines or any succulents.

WATER

WATER HAS BEEN a source of inspiration to people of many cultures for centuries. Even the simplest, most basic water feature can introduce a restful and refreshing element, while more extravagant fountains and cascades will excite the senses and invigorate the spirit. It does not matter where you live, whether you have a large or a small garden, whether it is newly laid out or has become well established over many years — water can add a pleasing and different dimension, often with the minimum of effort. Even the smallest apartment patio can usually accommodate a water feature of some kind.

There are endless possibilities, from a simple bird bath placed in a flower bed, under a tree or as a feature in a herb garden, to elaborate garden designs with extensive ponds and waterfalls. Whether created in a formal, natural or even a whimsical way, water adds an aesthetic element that no other medium can achieve. Apart from visual effects and the sounds it introduces, water also brings light and movement into a garden or patio area. A still, reflective pool will mirror images of buildings, plants, trees and any other features in the vicinity of the water, encouraging a mood of contemplation and a calm ambience. Moving water splashes and sparkles in the sunlight, adding life and vigor to the garden; and, of course, water also encourages birds and other wildlife, from frogs and toads to dragonflies.

The projects featured in this section are varied and range from a simple butyl rubber-lined bog garden to a formal fountain pool that requires good bricklaying skills. Ponds and pools may be combined and adapted to suit any garden style. There are several fountain ideas featuring a myriad of materials, from precast concrete to wooden barrels and flower pots and even bamboo fashioned the Japanese way — all are suitable for both gardens and patios, big and small.

IDEAS & INSPIRATION

For centuries, water has proven a marvellous medium for garden designers. In classical Rome, grand villa gardens were laid out with fountains and water channels; the Renaissance of the 16th and 17th centuries saw formal water gardens flourish in Europe; and by the 18th century, naturalistic lakes were being incorporated in great English landscape gardens.

Back to the Orient

Many people are inspired by ancient Oriental concepts. In China, water and rocks represent the feminine and yielding yin and powerful, masculine yang and feature prominently in Eastern gardens, while in Japan, water has long been treasured for the tranquillity it inspires. Many Japanese landscapers utilize even the smallest quantity of water to create inspired features – often with the inclusion of bamboo. The two most copied Japanese bamboo water features are the *tsukubai* and the *shishi-odoshi*, a traditional deer scarer. Traditionally, the *tsukubai* – a stone basin that is constantly filled with water through a length of bamboo

– has a functional use and is placed alongside the path leading to tea houses so that those entering may wash their hands. The *shishi-odoshi* was also developed for practical reasons – literally to scare deer and other wildlife. Water tips from one length of bamboo to another, which is pivoted, causing a see-saw action. The noise of the bamboo falling back against a striker rock is designed to frighten the animal.

Inspired by grandeur

Although grand locations can provide inspiration, water features should be in keeping with the size and style of your garden. Features in contemporary gardens are often showcased in magazines and are a good source of ideas.

Garden clubs and associations as well as some specialist magazines often organize visits to beautiful private gardens, many of which have ponds, pools, fountains and other water features that will certainly help you decide what to create.

Nature also provides enormous inspiration, particularly if you plan to create an informal pond or feature. Take note of natural streams and reflective pools; waterfalls in rocky grottos; cascades over rocks and boulders; meandering rivers. See how undisturbed stones and rocks feature in nature, and look carefully at the way plants grow in and around pools and along river banks. Then consider how you can use the many examples of nature.

Suitable styles

Having decided what appeals most, be sure that it will suit your garden. A shady corner on lower ground may

LEFT *A small, two-tiered pond is linked by a cascading waterfall; rocks around the edge create a natural effect.*

be ideal for a pond, particularly if water may naturally occur here. If there are already rock gardens and natural stone features in your garden, consider using stone for the water feature too. Incorporate a waterfall within a rock garden or extend rocks around the perimeter of the pond. If you have a stream running through your garden, this water may be harnessed to feed the water feature. Alternatively, the stream could be developed by peripheral planting and the addition of a bridge or perhaps even a viewing deck.

Fountains and symmetrical pools are generally more at home in the formal garden or courtyard, but the look can be varied by using different materials. A railway tie pool (*see pages 86–89*) can provide the same reflective qualities as a more formal pool, even though the rough timber and rendered surfaces are so different.

Trust your instincts

Spend time in your garden or on your patio, and try to visualize the completed feature. Note the wind direction and which areas are sunnier or more shaded than others. Sketch a scale plan of the area and the features you want to include. You do not have to produce a masterpiece – this is simply a way of assessing whether your plan will work and what will be required to make it work.

ABOVE *The* tsukubai *fountain traditionally served a functional purpose, the flowing water offering those entering a tea house the opportunity to rinse their hands.*

TOOLS, TIPS & TECHNIQUES

The skills required to build or create a water garden will depend entirely on the type of pond or feature you have in mind. On the simplest level, precast fountains and ponds provide a reasonably instant method that takes little time and effort. On the other end of the scale, more sophisticated or expansive ponds and water gardens require a variety of skills, from relatively simple carpentry to bricklaying and stonemasonry. Anyone who is able to appreciate fundamental building principles should be able to tackle all the projects featured on the following pages.

TOOLS

Other than standard bricklaying trowels, carpenter's levels and so on, there are no specialist tools required to build and create the water features, ponds and fountains detailed here. However, unless you are a regular do-it-yourselfer, there may be items that are not in your toolkit. Check the tools list prior to starting a project and, if necessary, borrow or hire what you do not have.

Basic items

You will need a sturdy builder's **wheelbarrow** (rather than a shallow gardener's wheelbarrow) to shift sand and transport bricks, railway ties and other heavy or cumbersome materials. **Picks, shovels, forks** and **spades** are essential for excavating ponds and pools, although you can probably get away with just a spade if you do not have to dig into heavy clay or move loads of stones. Not only is a spade the most common tool used for digging, it is also used for mixing mortar and concrete.

A retractable **tape measure** is another item no do-it-yourselfer should be without. Without a good-quality **steel tape**, you cannot set out projects accurately. When buying a new one, ensure that it has a locking mechanism so that you do no have to rely on someone else to assist you. Retractable steel tape measures are also invaluable when it comes to checking the depth of an excavated site as well as when working with other materials, especially timber.

Rakes and **brooms** are also handy items. A rake is invaluable for flattening out an excavated foundation and

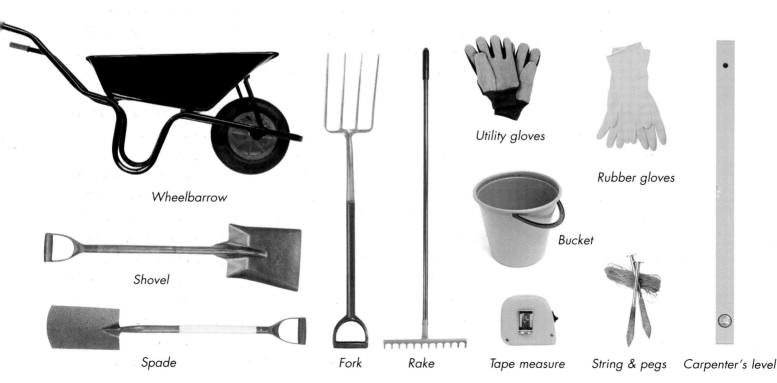

Wheelbarrow
Utility gloves
Rubber gloves
Bucket
Shovel
Spade
Fork
Rake
Tape measure
String & pegs
Carpenter's level

for removing loose stones. Apart from being useful for cleaning, a broom is the ideal tool to apply waterproofing compound to landscape fabric when this is used to seal a pond. Both paint (if the brickwork has been rendered) and waterproofing compounds will have to be brushed onto the surface, so ensure you have a selection of paintbrushes and at least one **bucket** handy.

Disposable gloves are useful when working with messy compounds. Thicker **utility gloves** made from leather are a good option when working with large rocks and stones. **Rubber gloves** are useful when working inside ponds that have already been filled.

Laying out

Projects may be laid out in a number of different ways. While professionals will generally stick to **pegs and builder's line** or **string**, it is sometimes quite adequate to use a length of garden hose or rope to define the area where a pond or pool is to be sited. If pegs are preferred, you can buy metal ones or simply make your own from stout sticks or thin lengths of timber. If you use wood, it helps to sharpen one end so the stick can easily be hammered into the ground. For smaller ponds and features, powdered **chalk** or **lime** may be sprinkled along the edges of the proposed site. Chalk or a carpenter's pencil can be used to mark the position of brickwork to be built on a concrete foundation.

An essential tool for bricklaying, a **builder's square** is also useful when laying out structures. Usually made from steel, these tools are placed at corners to ensure that brickwork forms exact 90-degree angles. They are really useful when laying out a square or rectangular pond, or when building a brick pool. A homemade square may be nailed together using three lengths of wood to form a right-angled triangle in the ratio 3:4:5. It can be as big or as small as required, but three lengths measuring 35½in (900mm), 4ft (1.2m) and 5ft (1.5m) will result in a square most do-it-yourselfers will find useful.

Levels

Levels are an indispensable aid. First on the list is a **carpenter's level**, which has vials for checking both horizontal and vertical surfaces. Various lengths are available; a shorter level can always be placed on a straight-edged length of wood to stretch across a pond or from one wall to another. A **straight edge** is also used to flatten and smooth the sand bed when paving around ponds and pools and it may be used to level and compact foundations. Marked off to indicate bricks plus mortar joints, it may also be used as a gauge rod to ensure that brickwork progresses evenly.

Although not specifically required for any of the water-feature projects that follow, a compact carpenter's square that incorporates a small carpenter's level vial is also useful.

A **transit level** may be used when leveling ground around the perimeter of larger water features, and is a suggested aid for construction of the koi pond (*see pages 106–109*). Equipment is set up on a tripod a short distance from the pond or pool, while a pole inserted in the ground at the edge of the excavation is marked to indicate a datum point – essentially the upper level required. A further series of pegs are inserted around the perimeter of the pool. One person looks through the lens of the level (which incorporates a carpenter's level vial), and visually lines up the datum point on all the pegs, indicating to a second person where to mark them. For a smaller pond, a carpenter's level with or without a straight edge, rather than a transit level, can be used to ensure that marker pegs are level.

While a transit level is expensive and used mostly by the professional builder or landscaper, a **water level** is remarkably inexpensive. Made with transparent tubing, it relies on the principle that water finds its own level. Instead of utilizing expensive professional equipment, the tubing is simply attached to a post in the ground and a datum point is established. Once the tubing has been filled with water, the other end of the tubing can be moved from point to point to track the horizontal level required. Peg and mark each of these points around the pond.

BRICKLAYING AND STONEMASONRY

A **large trowel** is used for spreading mortar, while a smaller **pointing trowel** helps neaten mortar joints. A **plasterer's trowel** has a flat rectangular side, used to smooth mortar onto a surface. Most professionals use a wooden float to smooth the mortar while it is still moist. **Corner trowels**, designed for inside and outside corners, will enable you to neaten all corners and outside edges.

Bricklayers and plasterers commonly use a large **metal mortarboard** or **hawk** to hold the mortar while working. This means using both hands at once; for the amateur, it is often easier to simply keep a supply of mortar nearby, in a wheelbarrow or bucket.

Builder's line or string used with homemade corner blocks – cut so that they slot onto the ends of the brickwork – is an indispensable aid when laying bricks along a straight line. This is moved up to the top of each course as building progresses, helping to ensure that the line of brickwork remains straight.

Use your carpenter's level to check that the bricks are level and the builder's square to make certain the corners are correctly angled.

Cutting

When using pond liners or installing fountains that require pipework, **sharp scissors** or a **utility knife** are essential.

Generally, only **handsaws** are required when installing and constructing water features, although a jigsaw, circular saw and even an **angle grinder** may be useful.

The **chisel** end of a brick hammer or a **brick bolster**, which has a wide blade, is ideal for bricks. A **brick hammer** (or mason's hammer) or a **cold chisel** used with a **stonemason's hammer** may be used on brick and stone, while an angle grinder can trim stone and cut bricks as well as stone and simulated stone edgings and paving.

Fixing & fastening

A **claw hammer** can knock in and extract nails, and may also be used with a **brick bolster** to cut bricks. You should also buy a set of good screwdrivers, or invest in a **spiral ratchet screwdriver** with interchangeable ends, as well as various bits for the **power drill** you will be using. If buying a new drill, consider one with a hammer action.

Various **wrenches** are used for attaching some of the fountain fixtures and fittings or bolts.

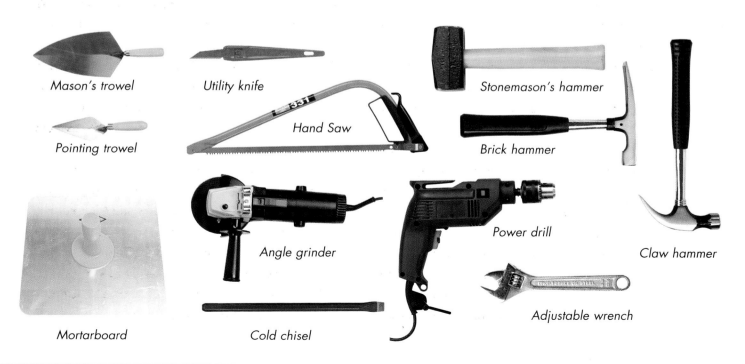

Mason's trowel

Utility knife

Stonemason's hammer

Pointing trowel

Hand Saw

Brick hammer

Angle grinder

Power drill

Claw hammer

Mortarboard

Cold chisel

Adjustable wrench

MATERIALS & CONSTRUCTION METHODS

A wide variety of materials may be suitable for building ponds, pools, fountains and other water features, but recast units may be used for freestanding features.

Clay & bentonite

Sodium clay creates an impervious pond lining, while **bentonite** is able to seal dams and reservoirs. Sold in powder or granular form, it is often mixed with soil and spread on the well-compacted shell of the pond, although the walls should never slope more than 1:3.

Specially manufactured **bentonite matting** can also do the job, but is more expensive. Two layers of landscape fabric material may be used to sandwich the bentonite in position.

Whichever method is used, never work in the rain. Once the soil and/or bentonite is compacted, it will take a few days for the water hydration process to take place and for the material to swell fully, thus sealing the pond.

Flexible liners

One of the simplest methods of lining a pond is to use a flexible liner. No special skills are necessary, although establishing correct levels is essential. Unfortunately, some liners puncture easily and not all types can be satisfactorily joined – which will affect the size of your pond.

Some people advocate padding the hole with soft sand or other insulation (even wet newspaper) first. As you fill the pool, the creases will stretch into the shape of the pond.

- **Polyethylene** is probably the cheapest, but it punctures easily and tends to deteriorate when exposed to the sun. Commonly used to damp-proof buildings, it is manufactured in various colors and different gauges. Black sheeting is used for pools as the carbon inhibits the effect of the ultraviolet. If you do opt for this, use a heavy gauge – at least 500 micron – and use two layers. Never use recycled polyethylene. Some manufacturers market a cross-laminated, high-density polyethylene for use with rubberized asphalt to join and patch material.

Butyl rubber

Landscape fabric

Polyethylene

- **PVC or vinyl lining** is unlikely to deteriorate as quickly as polyethylene. It is usually available in black or blue (which is the more common choice for those building swimming pools with a flexible liner). Since PVC can be heat-welded in the factory, it is suitable for quite large ponds. Laminated PVC has a textile reinforcing, which makes it reasonably strong and hardwearing.
- **Woven polypropylene** (which is plastic), as well as various landscape fabrics, may be used to line ponds if coated with a bitumen waterproofing compound. It is reasonably long lasting and, because the bitumen seals the surface, the base material simply has to be over-lapped rather than joined.
- **Pond-grade butyl rubber liner** (*see pages 70–73 and 82–89*) is the best quality flexible liner on the market, but it is also the most expensive. Available in various thick-nesses, it is highly resistant to puncturing and has more elasticity than the other liners. Black in color, it is said to have a life expectancy of at least 50 years, so if you want a pond that will be around a long time, it is worth considering. It has various other applications, but has been used to line canals and reservoirs for centuries.
- An **ethylene propylene polymer**, EPDM has largely taken the place of butyl rubber in some countries. Said to be UV-resistant and longer lasting than plastic liners, it is considerably cheaper than butyl.

Bricks & stone

Whether you choose to use brick or stone, you will need cement, sand and stone for foundations, and cement and sand for mortar. Ordinary building sand may be used for concretework and to bed paving units, but you will need a fine, soft sand for mortar. The mix should be no weaker than a 1:4 combination of cement:sand. Crushed stone is used for foundations, generally ¾in (19–20mm) in size. A smaller aggregate may be easier to work with, but you need to add more cement to the mixture.

Lime is toxic and can kill fish, so if you plan to stock the pond, use a non-toxic plasticizer to make the mixture more cohesive. If you use lime, leave to stand for three months.

A waterproofing additive will make mortar impervious to water. Products vary, so follow the manufacturer's instructions. Once the surface is dry, paint with a water-based, non-toxic bitumen sealant to prevent leaking. Moisture-curing polyurethane may also be used.

Stone ponds may also be rendered on the inside, or they may be fully or partially coated with fiberglass before being coated with bitumen.

Where holes need to be drilled into pond and pool walls to accommodate electric cables, be sure to seal these with a suitable silicone sealer.

Wood

While it may not seem the obvious option for creating a pond or water feature, wood can be wonderfully effective. Railway ties and wooden barrels are incorporated in some of the following projects (*see pages 86–89 and 102–105*). Railway ties also make an interesting surround to a pond, while timber slats are commonly used to construct decks adjacent to ponds or to create jetties.

In all instances, use only wood that has been treated, and if it is to be used to contain water, make sure that it is watertight. Old oak wine barrels were designed to hold liquid and swell when full, but railway ties will have to be lined with a flexible liner.

Rigid liners

Rigid liners may be installed above or below the ground, and installation is simple – provided the hole is the correct depth and level. Dig a hole slightly bigger than the liner and backfill with soil once it is in position. If a rigid liner is used above ground, incorporate a 'wall' to hide the sides.

- **Fiberglass** (glassfiber reinforced polyester) is molded by bonding layers of glassfiber with polyester resin. It is expensive and not always available in pond size.
- **Fibercement** ponds are not common and limited in size and shape. Comprising organic fibers and cement, they are lighter than concrete but heavier than fiberglass.
- **Precast concrete pools** are also molded and suited for use in courtyards or on patios. Some are available in a modular form, with several units slotting together.
- **Thermoplastic shells** are made from plastics such as PVC, and are only available in some countries.
- **Glassfiber reinforced cement** is rigid and is well suited to garden water features, such as informal ponds.

PUMPS & FILTERS

Pumps circulate water, while filters keep the water clean. Pumps are powered by electricity, but only low-voltage submersible units connected to a household circuit are used for these projects. The combination of electricity and water can be lethal, so if in doubt, call an electrician – especially if you need a separate circuit (for bigger projects).

Pumps and fittings are available from most nurseries and other specialist suppliers, and may also be safely and effortlessly installed. If cables are to be buried, use conduit or armored cable. Special weatherproof boxes may be mounted to walls, allowing you to plug the pump in at an outdoor spot, or the cable may be fed through a wall to an electrical supply inside the house or outbuilding.

The output of pumps is usually described in gallons/litres per hour, and is specified on the packaging. Dealers will advise which pump is best. Small, submersible pumps are generally simple to install and to operate – and they do not have to be primed. Most have a strainer on the inlet to prevent fish and floating debris from being sucked into the motor. Larger pumps are usually housed on the surface and these generally do have to be primed.

If you are installing a fountain, you will need to know how high above the fountainhead nozzle you want the water to reach. In the following projects, the water head (which is the height a pump can spurt from the surface of the water) is specified. Fountainheads vary in effect, from high-spurting geyser jets to dome or tulip jets. Decide which is most appropriate for your feature.

Although a filter is not essential for most ponds, if you plan to keep koi, it is advisable to install one since you will want to keep the water clear so that you can see the fish. A filter will also rid the water of harmful waste materials including dead plants, fish excreta and uneaten fish food.

Various filter types are available, the simplest being a biological filter box, which contains a combination of filter media – sometimes with the addition of several chambers with valves. Whatever type is chosen, it must have the capacity to keep the volume of water in your pond clean.

Although filters may be submerged in the water or housed outside the pond, the external type is more reliable and more accessible. Once in use, it needs to be disconnected at regular intervals to clean it. Always use pond water, rather than tap water, to clean a biological filter.

Fountainheads

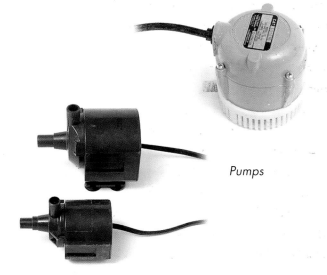

Pumps

NATURAL BOG GARDEN

CREATING A BOG GARDEN is inexpensive and not at all difficult; the secret is positioning it in a location that looks as if it could easily become waterlogged. Planted with species that thrive in boggy conditions, it will soon develop into a natural feature. Established alongside a pond or pool, a bog garden may be used to create a pleasant transition between water and land, successfully adding plant life, color and texture to the design. Created as a stand-alone feature, it may be as big or small as you wish.

2–3 HOURS

YOU WILL NEED

TOOLS
- spade
- utility knife and/or scissors

MATERIALS
- pond-grade butyl rubber sheeting:
  4ft x 4ft x ⅒in (1.2m x 1.2m x 2mm)
- crushed stone: 110lbs (50kg)
- irrigation tubing (optional):
  6½ft x ½in (2m x 12mm)
- selection of round river stones and pebbles
- selection of plants suitable for
  marshy conditions

A BEAUTIFUL BOG

A bog garden may be established as a natural extension to a pond or created as a feature on its own. Since a natural bog is quite simply an area of poorly drained ground, the ideal location is one that is naturally boggy. However, by utilizing a liner that traps water in the area defined for bog plants, this may not be a necessity. The tools required for the job are minimal and the only real requirement is creativity.

Once the construction of the bog garden is complete, the area is planted with any species that will thrive in boggy conditions. The perimeter of the garden is best defined with river stones to set it apart. If established alongside an existing pond, large stones may be used to successfully divide the two areas. Although this project calls for butyl rubber lining, ⅕in (0.5mm) PVC or at least 500-micron black polyethylene sheeting may also be used.

> **TIP** Since a bog garden must be kept moist, if your garden is large and you have an irrigation system, you may want to include the bog garden in the scheme. If so, perforate the tubing used within this section and do not use risers. The water will seep out into the bog garden and keep it damp.

1 Once you have found a suitable spot for your bog garden, excavate an area no less than 1¼ sq yds (1m²), to a depth of 8–12in (200–300mm). Keep the soil on one side as you will need to replace at least half of the soil later.

2 Position the lining in the hole and trim to the shape of your excavation. It is not essential that the liner extend to ground level as its function is to trap some water, rather than contain it. In any case, it should not extend above ground level.

3 Spread a thick layer of gravel or crushed stone over the base of the bog garden. This need be no more than about 2in (50mm) thick. If you are going to irrigate the area, lay the pipework now. It may either be attached to the irrigation system in your garden, or fitted with a hose connection at one end.

4 Plant with any species that will thrive around the perimeter of ponds or in marshland; lilies, flowering rush, marsh marigolds and irises are all suitable. Edge with round river stones to define the perimeter of the bog garden.

FORMAL FOUNTAIN POOL

THE SIMPLICITY OF the design of this raised pool makes it an ideal feature within a courtyard or on a formal patio. A precast fountain in the center of the pool adds character and charm, and introduces the soothing sound of running water. The freestanding fountain may be as plain or elaborate as you wish... from a simple bowl cascade to an ornate statue. Introduce color and texture by planting in and around the pool, or by placing interesting pots around the perimeter or on the raised walls.

YOU WILL NEED

TOOLS

- chalk or pegs and line/string
- corner blocks and line/string
- shovel and/or spade
- carpenter's level
- bricklaying and plastering trowels and floats
- mortarboard
- builder's square
- carpenter's pencil
- coarse-haired block brush
- paint brushes and buckets
- drill, with ⅓in (10mm) masonry bit

MATERIALS

- concrete: 400lbs (180kg) cement; 795lbs (360kg) sand; 795lbs (360kg) crushed stone
- bricks: 208
- mortar: 375lbs (170kg) cement; 1500lbs (680kg) sand; 80lbs (35kg) lime, or plasticizer
- waterproofing agent: ¼gal (1 l)
- bitumen waterproofing compound: 1gal (5 l)
- pipework: 3⅓ft x ⅝in (1m x 15mm) plastic irrigation pipe; 1 x elbow connector
- silicone sealant
- pump: immersible, 4½ft (1.4m) waterhead
- outdoor junction box with conduit as required

2 WEEKS

FOUNTAIN FEATURE

Only basic building skills are required to construct this simple 6ft x 6ft (1.8m x 1.8m) pool made from bricks and mortar. Once the structure is complete, the addition of a precast feature fountain, pot plants, statues and other characterful items simply require some creativity. The size and scale of the pool can easily be adapted to suit a different setting, and can even be constructed against a wall, incorporating a wall-mounted fountain rather than one that is freestanding.

The most important aspect of this construction is its ability to hold water and careful attention must be paid to waterproofing. Not only is a waterproofing agent added to the mortar used to render the inside surface of the pool, but once the plaster is dry, the inside walls are painted with several coats of a bitumen waterproofing compound. A moisture-curing resin could also be used.

To complete this project you will require bricklaying tools such as a carpenter's level, builder's square, various trowels and so on. No cutting of bricks is necessary. If you are in any doubt about electrical connections, leave this aspect to a professional.

1 Decide on a location for the pool and mark out a 6½ft x 6½ft (2m x 2m) foundation area with chalk or pegs and line. Dig out to a depth of about 4in (100mm) and check the level of the ground by placing a carpenter's level across bricks at various points.

3 Fill each of the holes left when the bricks are removed with concrete. Use a straight-edged plank to smooth the surface and then, with a chopping movement, compact the concrete until the water seeps to the surface. Use a plasterer's float or a trowel to smooth the surface and then allow to set thoroughly, at least overnight.

2 Mix concrete in the ratio 1:2:2 (cement:sand:stone), taking care to add only enough water to make the mixture workable. Leave about four or five bricks in the foundation trench and place the concrete in the trench. Use the upper surfaces of the bricks to gauge the thickness of the concrete, and carefully remove the bricks before the concrete hardens.

4 It is vital that the structure is both level and square. Use a builder's square to mark the corners of the pool with chalk or a carpenter's pencil before you lay even the first brick. You will need about 155lbs (70kg) of the cement for the mortar to lay the bricks. This should be mixed in the ratio 1:4 (cement:sand). Loosely lay the first course of bricks as a guideline, and then, working from the corner, lay a sausage of mortar about ⅜in (10mm) thick on the concrete foundation and flatten slightly with the trowel. Draw the towel lightly down the center of the mortar to create a small furrow to improve bonding. Then bed your first brick. Use the trowel to add mortar to the joints.

5 Build up the corner and use a carpenter's level to check both the horizontal and vertical surfaces.

6 To ensure that the corners progress evenly, lay a straight-edged piece of wood from one corner to the other and check the levels with a carpenter's level on top of the wood.

7 Set up the wooden corner blocks and builder's line in line with the wall's outside edge. This will help ensure the courses remain straight. As you lay the bricks, tap them firmly into place with the trowel handle.

8 Once one of the four walls has been built up to the required four courses, start laying the second, inner wall of brickwork. Butter the bricks and tap mortar into the joints with the trowel where necessary.

9 Continue building the double wall on all four sides, scraping any excess mortar off the bricks as you work. Allow the mortar to set, at least overnight.

10 You will need about half the remaining mortar mix to render (plaster) the outer surface of the brickwork. Mix the first batch of mortar. Dampen the brickwork before you start, as this will prevent the mortar from drying out too quickly. Use a mortarboard to hold the mix while laying it onto the brickwork with a plasterer's trowel. The trick is to apply just enough pressure to make it stick to the bricks.

11 The render must be ⅜–⅝in (10–15mm) thick. Use a carpenter's level to make two shallow vertical grooves to mark the surface.

12 Scrape excess mortar from the surface with a straight-edged length of timber, pulling firmly down over the surface. The finished surface should align with the base of the grooves.

13 Dampen the rendered surface by splashing with a thick block brush, and then use a wooden float to smooth the surface. Use even pressure, but do not over-trowel or the finer material will come to the surface and may cause cracking. Use a corner trowel to neaten the outside corners.

14 Sprinkle a little dry cement on the top surface of the walls. This assists adhesion of the mortar mix.

15 Spread the mortar across the upper surface with the trowel, pulling the trowel towards you.

16 Make grooves in the mortar with a carpenter's level in the same way as for the outside of the walls.

17 Use a carpenter's level and wood to check that the upper surface is still level. Then scrape the excess mortar off the surface.

18 Smooth the corner trowel along all the surfaces to neaten the edges of the structure. Mix the rest of the mortar, adding a waterproofing agent according to the manufacturer's instructions.

19 Render the interior surface in exactly the same way as you did the exterior walls. Neaten the inside corners with a corner trowel, and allow to set thoroughly.

20 Paint on a diluted coat of rubberized sealer according to the manufacturer's instructions. Three or four hours later you can paint on the first of two or three undiluted coats.

21 Drill through the base of the wall of the pool at a point closest to the electrical power supply.

Push 30in (750mm) of the pipe through the fountain, and then join the remaining 10in (250mm) length to the elbow. **22**

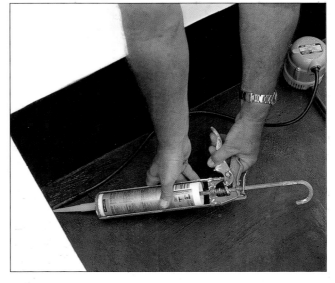

23 Position the fountain in the center of the pool and connect the pipe to the pump. Place it on the floor of the pool, next to the fountain.

24 You will need to remove the plug from the pump to push the cable through the hole you have drilled. Use the silicone sealer to seal around the hole once you have pulled the cable through. Connect to a power supply.

LILY POND

CONSTRUCTED PRIMARILY TO display a variety of aquatic and water-loving plants, this small lily pond will fit most garden styles. Grasses, ferns and rushes are planted alongside the pond, with a variety of marginal plants, including water irises, and floating plants within the water itself. A plain stone swimming pool coping around the edges defines the shape and finishes the pond off neatly.

1 WEEK

YOU WILL NEED

TOOLS

- shovel and/or spade
- straight-edged length of wood at least 8½ft (2.6m) long
- carpenter's level
- sharp scissors or utility knife
- trowel

MATERIALS

- pond-grade butyl rubber sheeting: 20ft x 4ft x ⅒in (6m x 1.2m x 2mm)
- resin and hardener
- paint brush
- coping stones: 24 stones x 10in x 10in (250mm x 250mm)
- mortar: 88lbs (40kg) cement; 265lbs (120kg) sand
- selection of suitable lilies and plants

POOLING RESOURCES

The shape and size of a pond constructed for plant life is really a matter of personal choice, but should be no smaller than this 4¾ sq yd (4m²) design. It may, however, be as large as you would like it to be. Shelves that are incorporated around the inner perimeter of the pond will enable you to position marginal and submerged aquatic plants in bags or other containers.

Pond-grade butyl rubber, the most favored of pond liners, has been used for this project. Not only is it long lasting and hard wearing, but pond-grade butyl rubber liner can also be joined together so that they form wider sheets. There are, however, a number of other options, from inexpensive polyethylene sheeting to harder wearing, laminated PVC. Similarly, the surround may be adapted; brick paving, a wooden deck or even a rock garden are options.

TIPS When filling a butyl-lined pond with water, do not try to stretch the rubber into shape – let the water do that for you.

When positioning plants on the shelves of the pond, use rocks around them to create natural containers and hide the edges of the liner.

1 Mark out the pond and excavate about 2in (50mm) deep. Decide whether you want shelves for marginal plants around the entire perimeter or just on one side. Dig the center of the pond to a depth of about 14in (350mm), ensuring that the sides do not slope too steeply.

2 You may need to join two or more lengths of pond-grade butyl rubber liner, but you will need a special resin and hardener to do this. Once mixed together, the resin is painted onto both sides, and allowed to dry until tacky. Then press the two sheets together carefully. Since different resins may vary slightly, be sure to follow the manufacturer's instructions.

3 Trim the edges of the pond back about 30mm (1¼in) to allow for the coping stones. Make certain at this point that the sides of the pond are level. Check the levels using a carpenter's level set on a straight-edged piece of wood placed across the pond.

4 Spread the rubber across the surface of the pond and let it fall naturally into the hole.

5   Fill the pond before you trim the edges of the rubber. Do not try to stretch the wrinkles out of the rubber as the weight of the water will gradually do this on its own.

6   Once the pond is full, trim the edges of the rubber.

7   Loosely lay the coping stones around the perimeter of the pond, so that they cover the perimeter of the rubber lining. If necessary, extend the shelf so that they fit.

8   Mix the mortar; put a little under each slab and fill the gaps using a trowel. Once the mortar dries, position your plants and watch nature take its course.

SHALLOW FEATURE POOL

MADE WITH RUSTIC railway ties, this shallow pool is reasonably formal in nature, but will fit in with most patio or courtyard styles. The impact of the final feature will be determined, to a large extent, by the surround — which may be grass, gravel, tiles, brick paving or even lush plants. The addition of a simple fountain feature in the form of a single upright tie, completes the picture. Alternatively, the pool may be constructed without the fountain to create a reflection pond; or the fountain may be erected alongside an existing pond.

1 DAY

TIP Before cutting ties, check the timber for old bolts and pieces of metal, and use an angle grinder for cutting rather than a power saw. If using a circular saw, you need a special blade to cope with hard wood.

REFLECTIONS OF RAILWAY TIES

Strength and tenacity are all that is required to create a shallow feature pool like this one. Railway ties are extremely heavy and difficult to cut; wherever possible, use existing lengths and be sure to have friends and family on hand to help when working with them. An advantage of the weight of this wood is that, except for the upright feature, the ties do not have to be bolted in any way to keep them in place. The lining should, however, be tacked or nailed to the wood to prevent it from sagging. Pond-grade butyl rubber liner is specified here, but PVC or black polyethylene sheeting (provided it has a thickness of least 500 micron, and is used in a double layer) may be an option here. You could also use a landscape fabric well coated with a good waterproofing compound.

YOU WILL NEED

TOOLS

- wheelbarrow
- spade
- rake
- carpenter's level
- straight-edged length of timber, at least 7¼ft (2.2m) long
- utility knife and/or heavy-duty scissors
- hammer
- drill, with wood bits
- wrench

MATERIALS

- sand: 22lbs (10kg)
- railway ties: 4 ties x 31½in (800mm); 1 tie x 35½in (900mm); 4 ties x 2.1m (6½ft)
- copper pipe: 12in x ⅝in (300mm x 15mm)
- pond-grade butyl rubber sheeting: 7ft x 4ft x ¹⁄₁₀in (2.1m x 1.2m x 2mm)
- galvanized nails: ¾in (60 x 20mm)
- galvanized metal bracket: right-angled, with 4 coach screws to fit
- flexible tubing: 31½in x ½in (800mm x 12mm) (internal diameter)
- pump: submersible, 4½ft (1.4m) waterhead

1 Level and clear an area of 7¼ft x 4½ft (2.2m x 1.4m) — slightly larger than the finished pool will be. Dig out the grass and use a rake to remove loose stones.

2 Top the excavated area with approximately 1in (25mm) of sand. Use a level or flat-edged piece of wood with a carpenter's level on top to compact and level it, drawing the level firmly across the surface towards you.

3 Use a wheelbarrow to move the railway ties as close to the site as possible. Position the first four ties, ensuring that they are at right angles to one another and are absolutely level. Sometimes, railway ties are slightly worn or they may be a little uneven; if so, use extra sand underneath to level them.

4 Once all four ties are in position, check across the width and length to make certain that all upper surfaces are still level. Where the carpenter's level does not span the length, use a straight, level piece of timber with the level on top.

5 Cut the pond-grade butyl rubber sheeting to size and then place it across the ties, tucking it in along the inside surfaces.

6 Nail the lining firmly to the ties, folding it neatly at all four corners.

7 Position the second layer of ties over the rubber edging.

8 Using the ⅝in (15mm) wood bit, drill a hole through the 35½in (900mm) railway tie, 8in (200mm) from one end.

10 Insert the length of copper pipe through the hole you drilled at the top of the upright railway tie.

9 Position the 35½in (900mm) tie at one end of the pool, in the center, with the drilled hole at the top. You will need to secure this tie to the upper surface of the tie behind it. Use a carpenter's level to ensure that it is vertical; place the metal bracket against the two ties and make four marks where it will be bolted. Drill holes for the coach screws using a suitably sized drill bit and then bolt to the ties with a wrench. Before tightening the coach screws, check again that the upright tie is vertical.

11 Slip one end of the tubing over the copper pipe at the back of the vertical railway tie and attach the other end to the pump. Connect the power supply and fill the pool with water.

JAPANESE BAMBOO FOUNTAIN

INSPIRED BY TRADITIONAL Japanese water features, this unusual design directs the water through three successive bamboo pipes and onto what appears to be a pile of round river stones. Concealed beneath the stones is a reservoir of water, which is constantly being pumped up through the right-hand bamboo upright to keep the water flowing. The same feature could also be constructed alongside a koi pond, so that the water flows constantly into the pond, or it could be a feature in a sand and stone garden.

YOU WILL NEED

TOOLS

- hacksaw
- sharp knife or chisel
- spade
- carpenter's level
- drill with various bits and extenders

MATERIALS

- bamboo uprights: 3¼ft x 3in (1m x 80mm) (outside diameter)
- bamboo spouts: 1 pole x 20in (500mm); 1 pole x 3¼ft (1m); 1 pole x 4¼ft (1.3m) (all 3in/80mm diamater, and with solid nodes at one end)
- sisal rope: 13ft (4m), soaked in water
- river stones: 30
- reservoir: sump or other suitable container; the non-porous plant pot used here is 12¼in (310mm) high and the diameter is 20in (500mm) wide at the top and 8¼in (210mm) at the base
- pipework: 5ft x ⅜in (1.5m x 10mm) piece of flexible tubing
- pump: submersible, 4½ft (1.4m) waterhead

1 DAY

BAMBOO IN THE BALANCE

The most challenging part of this project will probably be to find suitable bamboo. Ideally, it should still be green as the more it dries out, the more brittle it becomes. Some garden centers do stock bamboo; alternatively, you could try specialist suppliers or landscaping specialists.

Construction is reasonably simple: there are no screws or bolts and the various elements are tied together with sisal rope. The tricky part is ensuring that the three horizontal lengths of bamboo, which form the spouts, remain balanced. By cutting small notches out of the uprights at the points at which the two pieces of bamboo meet, you will prevent the bamboo from slipping.

TIPS Soak the sisal rope several hours before using. When it dries, it contracts and tightens.

If your drill extension is not long enough to penetrate the full inside length of the bamboo, use a long piece of metal with one sharp end, and tap firmly with a hammer.

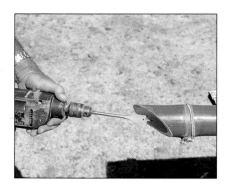

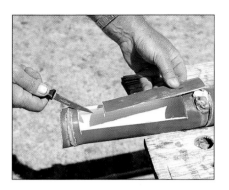

1 Cut the bamboo uprights and spouts to size using a hacksaw. Cut off the ends of all three spouts at an angle.

2 Leaving the bottom node of each spout intact, drill through the nodes down the center to hollow out the rest of each of the three lengths. Do the same to one of the uprights.

3 Place the 20in (500mm) length of bamboo on a surface with the longest edge face down. Using a sharp knife or chisel, cut out a rectangle about 7in x 2in (180mm x 50mm) — depending on the bamboo's thickness and distance between the nodes — between the two nodes. Repeat on the 4¼ft (1.3m) length.

4 Use a ¾in (19mm) wood bit to drill through the base of the 3¼ft-long (1m) bamboo spout.

5 Push the length of transparent tubing through the hole you have drilled in the bamboo.

6 Decide where to place the feature and dig a 12¼in (310mm) hole with sloping sides to accommodate the reservoir. The depth and shape of the hole can be adapted if your container has different dimensions. Place the reservoir in the hole, wiggling it around until it is straight and level. Check the upper surface with a carpenter's level to be sure. Backfill around the edges, taking care not to spill soil into the pot.

7 Dig two holes for the uprights, 23½in (600mm) apart. Position the two uprights in the holes and fill in with sand. Use a carpenter's level to check that they are perfectly vertical. Compact the soil around the uprights.

8 Cut a wedge out of the right-hand upright, ⅜in (10mm) from the top. Cut a wedge from the other upright, ⅜in (15mm) from the top. Someone will have to hold one end of the 3¼ft (1m) length of bamboo as you push the pipe through the hole in the right-hand upright. The pipe must extend to the base of the bamboo so you can pull it out and into the reservoir. A portion will remain underground. Tie the horizontal spout to the first upright, balancing the spout on the notch in the upright. Tie to the second upright.

9 Cut two more wedges in the uprights, 1in (25mm) below the first wedge on the right-hand upright, and ⅜in (15mm) below the first wedge on the upright on the left-hand side. Tie the longest spout onto the uprights at these points, using the cut-outs for support. You will need a third wedge on the right-hand upright to support the shortest spout.

10 Once all the bamboo has been secured with the sisal rope, connect the pipe to the pump and position the pump in the center of the reservoir.

11 Place the river stones over the pump and around the reservoir to hide it. Fill the pot with water before connecting the power and switching the pump on.

POT & FOUNTAIN FEATURE

IDEAL FOR THE corner of a patio, or simply to add interest to a blank wall, this water feature combines a wall-mounted fountain with a continually overflowing pot or urn. It takes up very little space and can be assembled in just a few hours, instantly introducing the sight and sound of trickling water. Many different ornamental fountainheads and masks suitable for mounting on the wall are available and any type may be used for this intriguing feature.

2–3 HOURS

YOU WILL NEED

TOOLS

- carpenter's level
- drill, with a masonry bit
- screwdriver

MATERIALS

- fountainhead: precast wall mask
- pot/urn: 22in (560mm) high and 10in (250mm) in diameter
- reservoir: sump or other suitable container; the waterproof plant pot used here is 12¼in (310mm) high, and the diameter is 20in (500mm) wide at the top and 8¼in (210mm) at the base
- putty: two-part epoxy putty
- bricks: 5 or more
- screws: 2 x 2in (50mm) brass screws, with Rawl plugs
- pipework: 6½ft x ⅜in (2m x10mm) piece of flexible tubing
- pump: submersible, 4½ft (1.4m) waterhead

DESIGNED TO FLOW

No special skills are required to create an attractive water feature similar to this one. While the lion's head is premounted onto a backing board, which is screwed to the wall, some fountainheads and wall-mask waterspouts are simply hung on a sturdy nail or bolt. If yours is a plastered (rendered) brick wall, you can hide the pipework by chasing into the wall to form a vertical channel into which the pipe is placed before the gap is replastered. For freestanding walls within the garden, another option is to drill right through the wall in line with the mouth of the mask and at the base, in line with the position of the pump. You can then run the pipe down the back of the wall where it is hidden from view.

When choosing a pot or urn, make sure it is waterproof. Many plant pots make ideal containers for water once the drainage holes have been plugged. The two elements should look as though they belong together; paint the two the same color or give them both a suitable paint finish, using a product that will weather well outdoors.

In addition to the pot and fountain, you will need a container to act as a sump or reservoir beneath the pot. Some pumps come with a sump; alternatively, use a plastic bucket or an inexpensive plant pot as seen here.

TIP River stones placed around the pot will hide the reservoir and create an attractive effect.

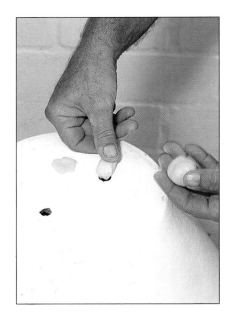

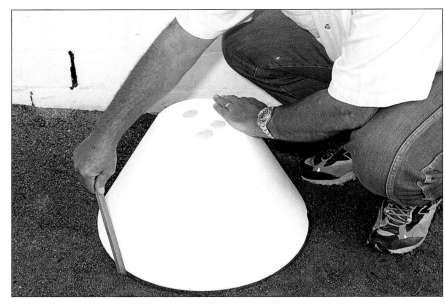

1 If you are using a plant pot with existing drainage holes, plug these with putty and allow to set.

2 Choose a suitable spot for the feature and mark out the position of the reservoir, no more than 8½in (220mm) from the wall. Dig a 12¼in-deep (310mm) hole with sloping sides to accommodate the reservoir (adapt the depth and shape to your container if necessary).

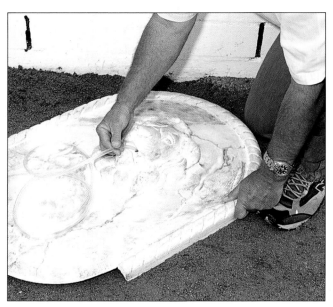

3 Position the pot in the hole and use a carpenter's level across the top lip to ensure that it is level. Carefully backfill any gaps around the outside of the container with soil and compact.

4 Before you screw the fountainhead or mask to the wall, insert the tubing through the mouth, allowing at least 8in (200mm) to protrude from the mouth.

5 Before attaching the fountainhead to the wall, mark where it will be positioned. You may need some help so that you can use a carpenter's level to check it is straight and to mark where the screws will go. Drill two holes in the wall at the marked points, but be sure to use a bit that is the correct size for the screws you are using. With the tubing still in place, screw the panel to the wall. The design of this panel ensures that there is a slight gap between it and the wall to accommodate the tubing. Make sure that there are no kinks in the tubing or the water will not flow freely.

6 Place a few bricks into the base of the container to elevate the pot to ground level. Connect the tubing to the pump and place the pump into the pot. There are various ways of plugging the pump into a suitable power point (see page 69).

7 Position the pot on the bricks, once again using a carpenter's level to ensure that it is level.

8 Fill the reservoir with water and place river stones around the feature. Fill the pot with water, connect the power and switch on.

MILLSTONE FOUNTAIN

ONE OF THE simplest, yet most effective water features you can include in any garden, big or small, is created with a single millstone or circular paving stone through which water is pumped to form a dome or bell shape. A selection of pebbles and round river stones add interest, at the same time camouflaging the reservoir of water below the stone. Colors and shapes should complement your own particular garden design, as should any planting you may choose to do.

YOU WILL NEED

TOOLS

- spade
- carpenter's level
- utility knife
- drill, with ½in (12mm) masonry bit

MATERIALS

- millstone: circular paving stone, 18in (460mm) in diameter
- reservoir: sump or other suitable container with a diameter of at least 4in (100mm) more than the millstone; the waterproof plant pot used here is 10in (250mm) high with a diameter of 22in (560mm)
- putty: two-part epoxy putty
- plastic flower pot: 8in (200mm) high
- selection of round river stones and pebbles
- pump: submersible, 27½in (700mm) waterhead and bell/dome fountainhead
- flexible tubing: 12in x ⅜in (300mm x 10mm)

4–5 HOURS

A SIMPLE SPRING

Simplicity is the key to this fascinating water feature, which requires more imagination than skill. In the absence of a genuine millstone, any concrete disc or round paving stone may be used. The fountainhead fitting you choose will determine the way the water falls onto the stone. While the dome or bell fitting is a favorite for the traditional millstone feature, for something different you could use a geyser fitting that spurts water relatively high into the air, or even leave the fountainhead fitting off and simply let the water spill gently over the stone.

Any suitable container may be used beneath the stone, provided that it is watertight and can accommodate a pot onto which the millstone may be placed. Alternatively, you could place a metal grid across the top of the reservoir and place the millstone on top of this.

> **TIP** When drilling the millstone, do this slowly on a solid, level surface to prevent cracking.

1 Once you have decided where to situate the millstone feature, place the container that will form the reservoir upside down and mark its position. Dig a hole 10in (250mm) deep. Fill any drainage holes in the container with putty and allow to set before placing in the hole. Use a carpenter's level across the top of the container to ensure that it is level.

2 Place the millstone on a solid and level surface. Then drill a hole in the middle of it, using a drill bit large enough for the hole you will need. This should correspond with the diameter of the pipe that connects the pump to the fountainhead fitting as the pump will have to be able to fit through the hole.

3 Using the utility knife, cut wedges from the top of the flower pot to allow water to flow freely. Make a hole in the bottom of the pot to accommodate the pipe.

4 Attach the pump outlet and tubing. Position the pump in the container and place the inverted flower pot over the top. Place the pot in the base of the container, ensuring that it is straight and level.

5 Carefully place the slab over the pipe, taking care that the pipework remains connected. The tip of the pipe should extend above the millstone very slightly (about ⅜in/10mm).

6 Place river stones around the plastic pot in the base of the container, taking care not to unbalance the millstone. try not to fill the reservoir with stones — you do need space for the water.

7 Fill the reservoir with water and slot the fountainhead fitting onto the tubing. Connect the pump to the power supply and then switch on. If the water spurts too high, trim the tubing and replace the fitting.

8 Now you can arrange stones and pebbles around the millstone so that the reservoir is completely hidden. This arrangement should be decorative and may include plants.

FLOWING BARREL

SIMPLE TO ASSEMBLE and perfect for a patio or uninteresting corner of the garden, this fascinating barrel feature has a rustic appeal and will look best in an informal environment. The same concept may be used in a formal garden, with pots instead of wooden barrels. In fact, any watertight container may be used, provided it has at least one drainage hole into which the pipework can be inserted.

1 WEEKEND

YOU WILL NEED

TOOLS
- drill, with a ¾in (19mm) masonry bit

MATERIALS
- railway tie offcuts: at least 4 offcuts x 15¾in (400mm); 8 offcuts x 23½in (600mm)
- oak barrels: 2 barrels x 12in (300mm) high x 15¾in (400mm) diameter
- silicone sealant
- garden hose: 5ft x ½in (1.5m x 12mm)
- pump: submersible, 5ft (1.4m) waterhead

GO WITH THE FLOW

The most difficult part of this project is to balance the top barrel at the correct angle to ensure that the water flows smoothly into the barrel on the ground. The only DIY skill required is the ability to drill a hole in the wood. Some kind of base is required to hold the angled barrel. Here railway tie offcuts have been used, but smooth-faced rocks and/or short logs would work equally well. If bricks or blocks are used, these will need to be camouflaged with plants.

The barrels used here were made from old oak wine barrels. Even though oak does expand when wet, ensure that the wood is thoroughly sealed before the barrels are put in place, otherwise the water may seep out and the water level will not be retained. If pots are used instead of barrels, these should be made from a non-porous material, or they, too, will have to be sealed. If you opt for ceramic pots, make certain they have at least one drainage hole through which you can insert the pipework; this option does not allow for drilling!

TIPS • Make sure the masonry bit you use is the correct size for the pipe you plan to insert. The pipe specified here has an internal diameter of ½in (12mm) and an approximate external diameter of ¾in (19mm).

• If the water does not flow smoothly into the bottom barrel, cut a slight groove in the top barrel to direct the water flow.

1 Check the base of the barrels and plug gaps in the wood with a silicone sealant. Once the silicone has set, fill the barrels with water and allow to sit for at least 24 hours. The water will make the wood swell. If they retain the water overnight and do not leak, they are watertight.

2 Use a flat wood drill bit to drill a hole in each barrel; at the edge of the base of one, and at the base of the sides of the other. Your pipework will go through the side of the bottom barrel and up behind the elevated barrel, through its base.

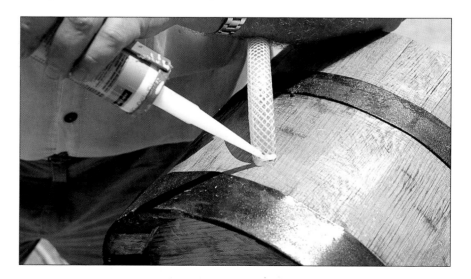

3 Insert approximately 8in (200mm) of pipe into the side of the barrel that will stand on the ground and then use silicone sealant to seal around the pipe to prevent water seeping out.

4 Use the railway tie offcuts to construct a base to support the top barrel. Position the second barrel on its side so that the bottom lip is tilted slightly upwards and insert the other end of the pipe in the hole drilled through its base. Since this barrel will not be filled with water, it is not necessary to seal around the pipe.

5 Attach the pump to the pipe in the first barrel. You can either camouflage the electric cable behind the flow of water, or drill a second hole in the bottom barrel and insert the cable through this. If the second option is chosen, the hole must be thoroughly sealed around the cable.

6 Once the silicone has set thoroughly, fill the bottom barrel with water before connecting the power to operate. You may want to plant around the feature so that it blends in well with the rest of the garden.

KOI POND

AN ATTRACTIVE, INFORMAL koi pond molded from concrete and joined with real rocks introduces a natural element to a corner of a suburban garden. Water is pumped over the highest point of the rock garden so that it flows down from the top pond to a smaller, deeper one below, adding both the sound and sight of water.

YOU WILL NEED

TOOLS

- rope and pegs
- shovel and/or spade
- carpenter's level
- bricklaying and plasterer's trowel
- sanding disc
- disposable gloves
- paint brushes and buckets
- transit level (optional)

MATERIALS

- cement: 1325lbs (600kg)
- sand: 70 cubic ft (2m³)
- crushed stone: 35 cubic ft (1m³)
- concrete blocks: 25 blocks x 15ft x 7½ft x 7½ft (390mm x 190mm x 190mm)
- bricks: 55
- rods: 19½ft (6m) x 12Y steel-reinforcing bar
- PVC sheeting: 14½ sq yds (12m²)
- wire mesh: 19 sq yds x ⅕in (16m² x 5mm) diameter
- waterproofing (cement additive): 3½gal (15ℓ)
- waterproofing: 2¼gal (10ℓ) bitumen (pond paint)
- oxides: 2¼lbs (1kg) dark brown; 2¼lbs (1kg) dark red; 2¼lbs (1kg) yellow (optional)
- fiberglass (to cover 8½ sq yds/7m²): 4½lbs (2kg) moisture-curing penetrating resin; 9½ sq yds (8m²) matting (chopped strand); 22lbs (10kg) general-purpose resin; 9lbs (4kg) top coat; 110gal (500ℓ) catalyst
- rocks: about 40 rocks and boulders of various sizes (70 cubic ft/2m³)
- pipework: 1 PVC pipe x 13½ft x 4½in-diameter (4m x 110mm); 2 bends x 90-degree x 4½in-diameter (110mm); 1 gully head and grate
- pump and filter: immersible pump with a waterhead compatible with the rockery height; biological filter
- electrics: outdoor cable and conduit; outdoor junction box

5–6 WEEKS

TRANQUIL WATERS

A fairly demanding project in terms of scale, this koi pond is on two levels and incorporates rocks and boulders. No two sites will be the same, but the principles used here may be adapted. If koi are to be introduced, a suitable pump and biological filter are an essential requirement.

No specialist tools are required, but sheer muscle is a prerequisite. Make sure you have help, particularly when it comes to shifting rocks.

Although not essential, fiberglass is used to seal areas under the rocks. You can seal the entire surface, but this is costly and time consuming. The moisture-curing resin is the same as is used to seal basements from damp, while the top coat is a non-toxic resin used to coat swimming pool surfaces.

Employ professionals to assist with plumbing and electrics. It is essential to install all pipework and fit electrical connections before you finish the pond and rock garden. Guidelines are provided on page 69.

1 Lay out the shape of the pond with rope or a garden hose. Stand back and try to imagine what it will look like once it is complete. If you are building on two levels, use two lengths of hose or rope.

2 Before digging, establish a datum point so you can mark the height of the surface around the pond by hammering pegs into the ground around the perimeter. Note the apex of the peg at the highest point and use a carpenter's level (or preferably a transit level) to adjust all the other pegs so that their tops are even. This pond is on two levels, so you need to establish two datum points. Dig the bottom pond to a depth of about 3¼ft (1m) in the center and the top one to no more than 12in (300mm).

3 Measure and cut the pipework so that it fits. (If you have no plumbing knowledge, employ a professional plumber to assist with the plumbing.) The weir will have to be located on the side of the pond, so dig a trench from the lowest point of the bottom pond to the weir. Place the pipes in the trench, with the gully head in the center of the pond. Refill the trench and compact.

4 Build a three-course wall of blocks between the two ponds, and incorporate vertical reinforcing rods in the blockwork. The water will flow from the top pool, over the wall into the pool below.

5 Lay plastic sheeting over the ground to protect tree roots from the cement, and then cover with wire mesh. Where the mesh overlaps, join with wire.

6 Mix concrete in batches in the ratio 1:3:3 cement:sand:stone, adding waterproofing agent according to the manufacturer's instructions. Throw the concrete over the wire mesh, lifting the mesh to allow some of the concrete to seep under it. Smooth with a plasterer's trowel as you work, and check and maintain the correct levels using a carpenter's level. Once both ponds have been concreted, allow the mixture to set.

7 Paint the moisture-curing resin on areas to be covered by fiberglass — in this case, those areas to be covered by rocks. When this is dry, paint with general-purpose resin and then stick the chopped strand over it according to the manufacturer's instructions. Paint more general-purpose resin over the top to saturate the matting. When the resin is thoroughly dry, sand the rough edges with a sanding disc, and then cover with a top coat.

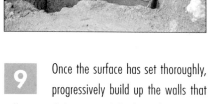

8 Mix mortar in batches and plaster over the fiberglass and bare concrete, thus rendering the entire surface. Allow to set overnight.

9 Once the surface has set thoroughly, progressively build up the walls that will surround the weir with bricks and mortar.

10 Start to position the rocks and boulders and, once you are happy, cement them into place using a 1:4 mortar mix.

11 Once all the rocks are in position, seal the surface of the bottom pond with the waterproofing compound. This has a black finish which is ideal for koi.

12 You may want to paint the top pond with bitumen; alternatively, mix mortar and waterproofing agent with oxide pigments and plaster to achieve a natural rock-hued finish.

A neat brick pathway defines and enhances the approach to the entrance of a house.

BRICK

THE OLDEST AND MOST universal man-made building material, brick has been used for hundreds of centuries to build walls, pave pathways and even construct stairways in the garden. Originally, bricks were not kiln-fired as they are today; instead, builders simply dried their bricks in the sun. The adobe bricks of Spanish America bear testimony to this traditional process.

Today, brick is probably the most widely used building material worldwide. Hard-wearing and attractive, it is certainly ideal for those who want to incorporate permanent structures within the garden. The decision to use brick may be determined simply by the structure you want to build and the obvious suitability of this material or, if yours is a brick house, by a desire to mirror the brickwork in the garden or on a patio, and so blend with an existing style. The size of the garden is unimportant; even the tiniest patio can accommodate a brick seat or a built-in planter, while large gardens invite seemingly endless possibilities. Structures built from brick range from the smallest plinth constructed to support a lamp to extensive garden walls and buildings. Built-in seating, tables and well-designed brick barbecues facilitate an outdoor lifestyle, while planters, ponds and pergolas have both a decorative and practical function.

Step-by-step projects included here are varied in both scale and style, from a relatively demanding barbecue structure and an interesting screen wall, to several smaller, more decorative features. In addition to structures, the building of a brick-paved path has also been detailed here, so that garden floors may also be covered with this versatile material. Even though projects are quite specific in terms of the feature being constructed, the basic methods used to build pillars, planters, steps and walls may all be utilized in a variety of different ways, enabling you to create just about any garden structure or feature imaginable.

IDEAS & INSPIRATION

Some of the most romantic and beautiful vistas in today's gardens incorporate bricks: old brick walls, discolored and crusted with moss; enticing moon walls that beckon visitors through a hole in the bricks to landscapes beyond; well-worn paths that seem to have been around for decades.

In the early days of brick, when clay was simply molded and left to dry in the sun, walls weathered and deteriorated far quicker than they do today. Over the centuries, as technology improved, ways were devised to fire bricks under intense heat to make them tougher. Techniques were also found to decorate them by glazing, embossing and coloring. Even traditional adobe bricks, made from mud, are stabilized with asphalt to make them impervious to water. Today, bricks are available in many earth-hued colors, with a number of finishes, from smooth to rustic stone-faced. A variety of copings is also available.

ABOVE *Brick walls and steps give structure to an informal garden.*

ABOVE *Curves can soften the often hard lines of brickwork.*

Establishing a pattern

Bricks are laid so that they bond together for strength, and by the time they were manufactured as standard units a number of bonding patterns had been established. The so-called English bond, used to construct double-thickness walls, comprises alternate courses of bricks laid along the wall (stretchers) and bricks laid across the width of the wall (headers). The Flemish bond, on the other hand, consists of complete rows of stretcher and header courses laid in each course, creating a geometric pattern. Several bonds, now known as garden-wall bonds, were once used only for boundary and screen walls. English garden-wall bond is a variation of the English bond, but with fewer header courses, separated by three to five stretcher courses. Flemish garden-wall bond consists of a header followed by two or three pairs of stretchers (rather than just one) in the same course. Today, however, bond patterns are far more straightforward and it is often the additional features that give these brick structures their character and charm.

Making a choice

The choice of which brick and which bond to use will depend largely on personal preference; but the kind of wall you are building will also affect this decision. A wall to be smothered with creepers or fronted with shrubs and flowers does not need a complicated bond pattern. Consider incorporating planters and alcoves, even seats and ponds. The wall may provide a perfect backdrop and will break the monotony of unbroken brickwork.

Many acclaimed landscape gardeners favor wild woodland gardens, but often include brick-piered pergolas in their designs, because the simple but elegant structures are an ideal support for climbers, creepers, roses and vines. Eventually, the wooden slats become entwined with the plants to create a shady bower. Professional garden landscapers also use brick paving, for instance, as part of a geometrically planted garden, and less formal styles.

Paving the way

Like walls, bricks used for garden floors are laid in bond patterns, each of which gives a different look and feel. Similar to stretcher bond, running bond is quick and easy to lay. Herringbone, which may be laid diagonally or at right angles, is strongest and one of the most attractive. Other materials, including concrete and wood, are often introduced to form decorative edgings. Magazines and books are a great source for ideas, but your own garden is likely to be quite different from those that inspire you. Try to visualize what the paved areas will look like in your own garden and which patterns will best suit the surround.

Finally, remember that good design is essential to any garden scheme. If you choose to use brick, make sure that the color and finish suits the style and finish of your house and that it blends with the garden itself. Plan carefully and be sure to follow all the basic building rules.

ABOVE *An expansive entertainment area may be paved in steps that gradually lead up to an open patio.*

TOOLS, TIPS & TECHNIQUES

There are few principles you have to learn to be able to lay bricks properly, but the basics are all essential. If a brick structure is not square, level and plumb, it will appear lopsided and could even collapse. Adequate foundations must be thrown and the mortar used to bond the bricks must be correctly mixed. It is also essential to work cleanly as excess mortar will stain brick surfaces. Other than that, all it takes is practice – and practice makes perfect.

TOOLS

The basic toolkit for brickwork is not extensive, but it is quite specific. Apart from a tape measure and trowel, other tools will help you ensure that what you are building is square, level and plumb. You will need a range of basic items, and if the structure includes timber, you will need woodworking tools including saws, drills and so on. Only the basic items and bricklaying tools are considered here.

Basic items

Since all brick structures require a foundation, a certain amount of excavating is unavoidable. You will need a **spade**, preferably a **shovel** for mixing concrete and a pick for digging into hard ground. A good-quality builder's **wheelbarrow** with a pneumatic tire is also essential, not only for carting bricks and materials from place to place, but also for mixing small quantities of concrete and mortar.

All brickwork needs to be built on a stable foundation, and both earth and hardpan need to be compacted. For larger jobs, including paved patios, it is best to hire a **compacting machine**. Alternatively, a homemade **tamper** can be made: insert a pole in an empty 1 gal (5 l) paint can and fill it with concrete. Once the concrete sets, the pole forms a handle and the tin the base of the ramming tool. For small jobs, a hefty pole does the job just as well.

Before you start, you need to measure and mark a foundation area. A retractable **tape measure** is invaluable.

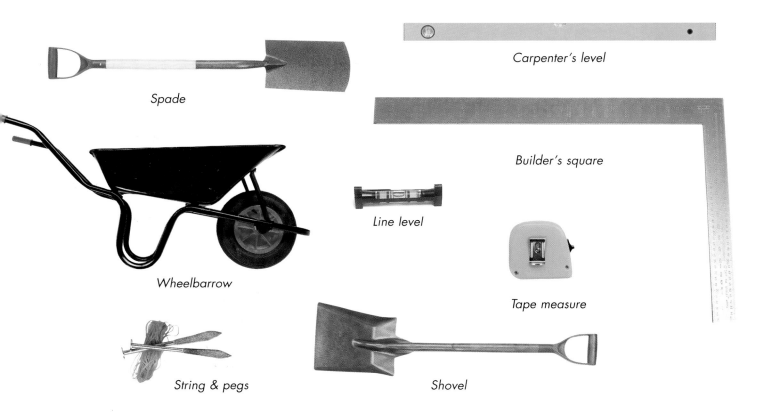

Spade

Carpenter's level

Builder's square

Wheelbarrow

Line level

Tape measure

String & pegs

Shovel

Bricklaying tools

Builder's line or **string** is used from the setting-out stage, where it is used with **pegs** or even **long nails** (*see page 156*) and throughout the building process. During brick-laying, it is used with either corner blocks or special metal pins to identify the upper level of the course of bricks. While some builders simply wind the string or line around a brick to secure it, the pins and corner blocks do allow you to mark the building line more accurately. Homemade **corner blocks** are the cheapest option; these are cut from two offcuts of wood approximately 4in x 2in x 2in (100mm x 50mm x 50mm). A section is cut from each to form a chunky L-shaped device into which a slot is sawn to hold the string. The block is then hooked onto the corner of the brickwork at the correct height, and the line stretched to the opposite corner of the wall, and the second corner block.

A **gauge rod** – essentially a straight-edged length of timber marked off according to the height of several brick courses, plus a mortar joint – is another useful homemade tool. A useful trick is to mark off the first few courses on a straight edge, and then to use this to ensure the rest of the brickwork is consistent.

The two essential tools that will enable you to ensure that the brickwork is plumb, level and square are a **steel builder's square** and a **carpenter's level**. The square is similar to a mathematical tool but much bigger and this will enable you to check that corners have the required 90-degree angles. Since a square is marked off like a ruler, it may also be used instead of a tape to measure on small areas. But apart from a **mason's trowel**, the carpenter's level is probably the most valuable tool for bricklaying. Without it you simply cannot check to see whether horizontal and vertical levels are flat and plumb. Made of metal, a carpenter's level incorporates both a vertical and horizontal vial containing a spirit-based liquid; if the bubble in the vial is in the center, the surface is level. If the bubble is not centered, you will need to re-lay the brick.

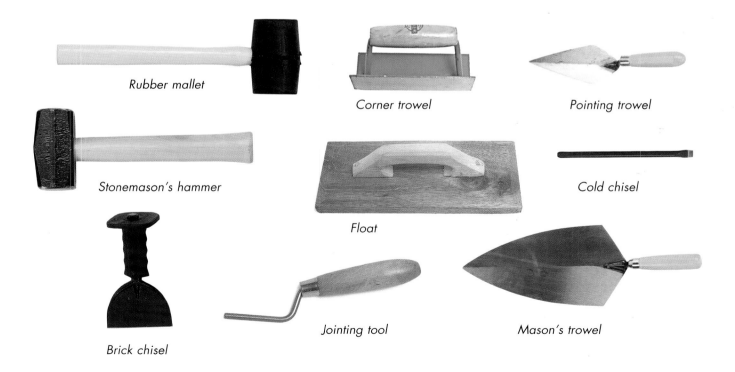

Rubber mallet

Corner trowel

Pointing trowel

Stonemason's hammer

Float

Cold chisel

Brick chisel

Jointing tool

Mason's trowel

When you are laying a reasonably long wall, a **line level** (basically a vial without the metal casting) may be strung on the line between your corner blocks and used as an additional aid. Unlike a carpenter's level, the line level can only be used to check the horizontal surface and cannot be used to check for plumb (vertical surface). Nevertheless, it is an invaluable tool.

When it comes to the actual job of laying the bricks, you will of course need a **mason's trowel**. If you are going to render (or plaster) the walls, you could use a **mortarboard** (or hawk) to hold the mortar – although many DIY bricklayers simply scoop the mortar up with the trowel as and when they need it.

You will also need a **float** to smooth the rendered surface. If you are plastering, it is also a good idea to include **corner trowels** in your toolkit; without them, you will never achieve a really professional finish. Shaped to fit either inside or outside corners, these tools are used on the vertical edges of a structure that has been rendered with mortar and simplifies the task of neatening these tricky areas. If you are building a facebrick wall you should use a **jointing tool** to rake out excess mortar; however, a piece of metal also works quite adequately on smaller projects.

A **pointing trowel** (which looks rather like a small-scale bricklayer's trowel) may also be used to fill in the mortar between bricks, but this is an optional extra for the DIY builder. Do not be tempted to use fingerwork for either job; cement can damage your skin.

The only other tools you are likely to need are those required to cut the bricks and, for paving, a **rubber mallet** to tap any protruding bricks into place. The simplest way to cut a brick is with a **bolster** and a **stonemason's hammer** as the thick blade of the bolster should enable you to break it in one go, without damaging or breaking the brick. The **chisel** end of a **brick hammer** may also be used, but this does tend to break the brick unevenly if you are not adept at handling the tool.

MATERIALS & CONSTRUCTION METHODS

The materials used for brickwork are quite standard, even if they vary in detail. They include a variety of different bricks and blocks, which are laid on a concrete foundation (made with cement, sand and a coarse aggregate like crushed stone, also mixed with water) and bonded with mortar (cement mixed with sand, water and sometimes lime or plasticizer). Metal reinforcement may be required for larger structures; and other materials, including wood for benches or simulated stone (made from precast concrete), may also be incorporated in brick features.

Bricks and blocks

A variety of building units made from clay, concrete or calcium silicate are usually available in a reasonable range of sizes. The general choice will be between units that are made to be rendered with mortar, and those that are fired to achieve an attractive face. While some precast concrete blocks are hollow, a lot of bricks are solid. Some may have indentations (sometimes referred to as a frog) on one face, or they may have two or three holes through the center of them. Frogs aid bonding of the bricks, as do the holes, which are formed during an extrusion process of molding the bricks.

Some bricks and blocks are shaped, either to finish walls and create copings, or for use as pavers; others are fired to extreme temperatures for special use. **Bullnosed bricks**, which are rounded at one end, are manufactured specifically for use around the edge of pools and ponds. **Firebricks** are a good choice for the cooking surface of any barbecue structure, and tough engineering or **exposure-grade bricks** are the best option if bricks are likely to be exposed to constant damp, around a pond, for instance. The quality of bricks does vary and you may find that there is some variation in the size and finish of different facebricks available in the trade. Suppliers in your particular area will be able to provide specific information.

When laying bricks, there are accepted configurations (and terms) which are universal. For instance, one single row of bricks laid lengthwise, with the next course overlapping by half a brick, will result in a 'half-brick' wall laid in a stretcher course. This is one of the most common designs for modern garden walls. (A one-brick wall requires a double layer of brickwork which, in fact, measures one brick across its width.)

Often, the coping on top of the wall is also brick, and the simplest variation can add surprising interest. For instance, bricks may be laid on edge, long sides together, to form a header course along the top of the wall; or they may be laid on edge to form a slightly narrower stretcher course along the vertex of the wall. Another alternative is to lay the coping in an upright soldier course; or side by side to form an even thinner sailor course, where the ends rather than the upright face sections abut.

Step-by-step photographs illustrate quite succinctly how to lay bricks for the various projects. The technique is not difficult; it may just take a little practice to master. The first step is to lay the first course accurately. Lay a sausage of mortar on the foundation and create a jagged groove through its center with the trowel. Then push the brick firmly into the mortar, so that it is level. If you can quickly master the art of buttering the smallest end of the brick with mortar and then sliding it into place and knocking it down so it is level with the first brick, you are ready to tackle just about any building project. The professionals do work fast, but do not try to imitate them until you are certain that all your levels are correct. Rather take a week to build a 3¼ft (1m) wall than have to knock it down because it is crooked.

When it comes to laying bricks in the garden, thinner brick pavers are usually better (although ordinary bricks will also make a perfectly acceptable, slightly thicker – and more expensive – patio surface). Whatever the choice, bricks used for paving may either be laid in a thick bed of sand or in mortar on a concrete base. The more solid option is more common for driveways than patios.

Autumn facebrick

Autumn paving brick

Cored facebrick

Granite facebrick

Concrete block

Concrete & mortar

In addition to water, the two materials common to both concrete and mortar are cement and sand. In both instances, ordinary Portland cement is used internationally. Sold in 110lbs (50kg) – and sometimes also 55lbs (25kg) or 90lbs (40kg) pockets – cement must be carefully stored. If it gets wet, it will become lumpy or solidify and will not be useable, so do not buy more than you need for any one project, and always discard hard or lumpy cement.

Only clean, graded sand should be used for mortar and concrete. Commercial sand suppliers sell evenly graded sand often suitable for both purposes. If you are faced with the option of 'soft' or 'sharp' sand, use the soft sand for mortar mixes and the coarser, sharp sand to mix concrete. Remember that sand that does not contain sufficient fine material (usually referred to as 'fines') tends to produce a weak, porous layer if used for concrete. If the sand used for concrete is too fine, the cement will probably rise to the surface. In some areas, 'plaster' sand is also available. This sand generally includes some lime and is a good choice for both bricklaying and for the mortar to be used to render walls.

Even though the source of sand is not a foolproof guide, river sand is generally clean and may contain hard, rounded stones that increase the workability of the concrete. A disadvantage, however, is that the fine particles have often been washed out by the river water. Beach sand almost always contains shell particles and salt, and if it is to be used for building work, it should have been thoroughly washed and graded by the supplier (who must, of course, have quarried the sand legally). Be sure to avoid fine wind-blown sands from desert areas and mine-dump sand (which also tends to be fine and generally too uniform for building use).

Coarse river sand

mortar

Crushed stone

Small stone chips

Various coarse aggregates, including gravel, natural pebbles and crushed stone, may be used to give bulk to concrete. The aggregate sold commercially is generally screened to what is referred to as 'single sizes'. A popular size for DIY projects is a ¾in (19mm) aggregate, although a smaller ½in (13mm) stone may be easier to work with. The larger of these two sizes is presumed to be the choice for concrete in all the projects featured. Certainly, the smaller stone is easier to work with but if it is used, slightly more cement should be added to the concrete mixture.

Both sand and crushed stone are usually available from stores that supply builders' materials. Alternatively, these materials may be ordered in bulk and delivered by the truckload, in which case larger quantities will have to be ordered.

For those DIY builders who need minimal quantities, premixed materials may be used for both concrete and mortar. This option is particularly useful when building small features. Although the mixing ratios are not always specified on the packaging, the general use for which they were intended usually is.

Available at the same outlets that supply premix, cement and loosely bagged sand and stone, as well as hydrated builder's lime, are available in 55lbs (25kg) pockets. A useful additive to mortar mixes, lime will improve the cohesiveness of the mix and help retain more water. It will also help prevent the mortar from cracking once it has set. A liquid plasticizer may also be added to mortar to make it more workable.

Mixing concrete and mortar is an art in itself. First and foremost, you will need to develop a knack of knowing how much water to add to the dry materials. A safe rule of thumb for mortar that is to be used in the garden is to stick to a 1:4 (cement:sand) mixture. Mix the dry materials first and then slowly add a little water until it is moist but not runny.

Concrete is mixed in exactly the same way, only the stone does make it more difficult to combine all the materials. When mixing by hand, do not try to mix all the

concrete at once; instead, mix a series of smaller batches. Start by combining the sand and cement, and then add the water gradually, shovelling the dry materials into the center until the mix is soft and smooth. Add the stone last.

Most of the following projects call for a concrete mixture based on a ratio of 1:4:4 of cement:sand:stone (mixed by volume). A slightly weaker mix may sometimes be suitable and, in some instances, a stronger concrete may be advisable – if, for example, the foundations are to support a solid brick wall. For some of the projects, a more specific water ratio has been suggested. However, once you are more familiar with working with mortar, you will soon know when enough water has been added to the dry materials to make it workable, and this is what is really important.

Only a couple of projects call for rendered surfaces, but this is an option that may be adapted to just about any brick feature. Mortar is usually mixed in the same ratio as for bricklaying, so the two compounds are compatible. Even if lime or plasticizer was not added to the bricklaying mortar, it is a good idea to add it to mortar used for rendering as it really does make it more pliable. Adding of a bonding agent will also ensure that the mortar sticks to the surface to be rendered.

Reinforcing

Garden structures seldom require much reinforcement, but some concrete footings and pergola pillars may need to be reinforced with metal rods, strapping or hoop iron. The metal is usually set into the footing and may extend to the top of the structure.

Sometimes, **light mesh or a metal grid** may be required in the foundation trench or you may have to set vertical steel bars into concrete. These steps are usually taken on the advice of an engineer.

The most common form of reinforcing incorporated into brickwork is **wire mesh**, available in rolls, and laid over the horizontal plane of brick courses. It is most useful when reinforcing the upper surface of small openings in walls.

BUILT-IN PLANTER

A PLANTER CONSTRUCTED under a window creates a raised bed that, when planted with annuals, adds a splash of color to an otherwise dull and uninteresting space. Similar planters may be built alongside garden walls or even as freestanding structures on different levels of the garden. They may also be included in the layout of an outdoor stairway or built on either side of steps or at the entrance to the house.

YOU WILL NEED

TOOLS

- shovel and/or spade
- chalk or lime
- tape measure
- carpenter's level
- builder's line or string
- brick and plastering trowels
- wooden float
- cold chisel and stonemason's hammer
- paint brushes

MATERIALS

- concrete: 44lbs (20kg) cement; 175lbs (80kg) sand; 175lbs (80kg) stone
- bricks: 48, two of which are halved
- mortar: 44lbs (20kg) cement; 175lbs (80kg) sand; 2¼lbs (1kg) lime or plasticizer (optional)
- paint
- waterproofing compound

3–4 DAYS

A BED OF BRICKS

A very simple project to tackle, this planter requires only the most basic bricklaying skills, and is ideal for the novice builder. If you follow the step-by-step directions very closely, and build the planter alongside the house or an outbuilding, be sure to match the finished surfaces. If yours is a facebrick home, choose bricks that match the building and do not render the finished surface. The finished planter should also be in proportion to the adjacent building. This planter is 5½ft (1.7m) and a little less than 27½in (700mm) deep; it stands 10in (250mm) from the ground.

If you decide to build the planter as a freestanding structure, you will need additional bricks for the back wall, as well as extra mortar for bricklaying.

TIP If a brick is too high, knock again firmly with the trowel handle. If it is still higher than the other, lift it and remove a little of the mortar.

1 Measure and mark the area where you plan to build the planter. Here a rectangle of 6ft x 31½in (1.8m x 800mm) is marked out adjacent to the house using chalk.

2 Dig a 12in-wide (300mm) 3in-deep (75mm) trench on the inside of the pegged lines. Remove any vegetation from the area.

3 To prevent the concrete spilling into the center of the planter, loosely lay bricks in the trench. Mix concrete in the ratio 1:4:4 with a little water and lay it in the trench you have dug. When the concrete has set, remove the bricks from the inner trench.

4 Mix half the mortar in the ratio 1:4 (cement:sand), adding lime or plasticizer if required. Lay a ⅖–⅗in-thick (10–15mm) sausage of mortar along the line where the first couple of bricks are to be laid and use the tip of the trowel to create a furrow.

5 Bed the first brick in the mortar, pressing it firmly in place. Tap with the handle of the trowel to ensure that it is properly embedded. Use a carpenter's level to ensure it is perfectly horizontal.

6 It is vital that all corners are at right angles. Use a builder's square to check the corners before you complete the first course of the front wall. They must be at 90 degrees.

7 As building progresses, it is a good idea to string a line across the front wall to help keep it straight and level. Use pegs or simply wind the string around a brick and place this on a pile of bricks. Also continue to use the carpenter's level at every stage.

8 If there are any gaps between the bricks, lift a little mortar onto the trowel and use a chopping motion to point (or fill) these spaces. Be sure to scrape any excess mortar off the surface of your brickwork as you work.

9 You will need to cut two of the bricks in half as half a brick is used in each course. Place the brick on the ground and score the surface to mark a cutting line. Place the chisel blade on the line and knock firmly with a hefty stonemason's hammer.

10 Mix the balance of the mortar and then render the surface (*see page 121*). Remember to press down firmly to ensure adhesion to the brickwork. Once the surface is reasonably level, use a wooden float to smooth it out.

11 Once the mortar has set properly, you can paint it. If the planter is adjacent to the house, before you fill the planter with soil, paint on a waterproofing compound to ensure that moisture does not seep through the walls and cause damp on the interior walls of the house.

CIRCULAR PLANTER

A SIMPLE, CIRCULAR planter can add new height and interest to an area that is not suitable for a flower bed. The color and texture of facebricks may be in keeping with stone features and rock gardens elsewhere in the garden. Alternatively, more affordable bricks can be plastered and painted in a variety of colors. This design is versatile: use it as a feature, or around a tree you may want to isolate for aesthetic reasons.

1 WEEKEND

YOU WILL NEED

TOOLS
- shovel and/or spade
- tape measure
- carpenter's level
- trowel

MATERIALS
- concrete: 55lbs (30kg) cement; 330lbs (150kg) sand; 150kg (330lbs) crushed stone
- facebricks: 64
- mortar: 35lbs (16kg) cement; 140lbs (64kg) sand; 17½lbs (8kg) lime or plasticizer (optional)

CIRCLES IN THE SAND

The size of the circular planter will be determined largely by the scale of your garden or the area in which it is to be sited. This one has been set back towards a bank earmarked as the perfect site for a rock garden – allowing for the inclusion of flowers in an area where both soil and location are less than ideal for bedding plants.

Only the most basic bricklaying tools are necessary for this project and the skills needed are minimal. You do not even have to cut any bricks. The most important aspect is to ensure that your circle remains round as you lay your first course. Once this first course is in place, common-sense building principles (level and plumb) are all you need to complete the circle. The materials required are also minimal as there is no need for a hefty foundation and a reasonably weak mixture may be used. Do not lay concrete in the middle of the planter as you will need ample drainage for the plants.

TIP When laying out a circle, use a basic compass made with pegs and string the length of the radius of the circle. Knock one peg into the center of the circle; attach the string to it and then rotate the string, marking the circumference as you do so.

1 Decide on a suitable spot for the planter and roughly mark out a circle with a diameter of approximately 4½ft (1.35m).

2 Remove the grass or any other vegetation and dig away surplus soil to create a flat base.

3 Place the 16 bricks to be used to build the first course in a circle on the ground exactly where you are planning to build the planter. Then place a carpenter's level across the bricks and check levels at several points. The more accurate you are at this stage, the easier it will be to build the planter properly.

4 Remove the bricks and dig a 8in-wide (200mm) and 8in-deep (200mm) trench around the perimeter of the area cleared for building, starting about 2in (50mm) to the outside of the circumference of the circle. Mix concrete in 1:5:5 with 22gal (110 litres) water for every 220lbs (100kg) cement and place in the trench.

5 Use a wooden float to compact the concrete and level it off. Use a carpenter's level to check the upper surface. Allow to set thoroughly.

6 Put the 16 bricks back into place without mortar, leaving ⅖–⅗in (10–15mm) gaps between each one. They should all remain here until they are laid in mortar to help ensure that your circle stays round.

7 Mix the mortar in the ratio 1:4 (*see page 121*) and remove one brick. Place a blob of mortar on the concrete to form a sausage shape; use the tip of your trowel to push it down and make a jagged furrow through the center of it.

8 Bed the brick in the mortar and use the trowel handle to knock it firmly into place. Use a level to make certain it is flat and level.

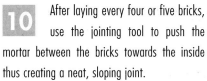

10 After laying every four or five bricks, use the jointing tool to push the mortar between the bricks towards the inside thus creating a neat, sloping joint.

9 Continue laying all the bricks in the first course. There is no need to butter the ends of the bricks in the usual way as the joints will be a lot thicker towards the outside of the structure. Instead, push mortar between the joints and neaten with a jointing tool (*see also Step 10*). Once the first course is complete and neat, lay the second course to form a stretcher bond.

11 Regularly check the upper surface of your bricks across the diameter at different points to make certain that they do not lean at an angle. If you do not have a long level, use a short one on a straight edge. Lay all four courses using a stretcher bond and allow the mortar to set well, preferably overnight.

12 Fill the planter with good-quality potting soil and plant seedlings or shrubs.

BARBECUE NOOK

THIS INGENIOUSLY SIMPLE brick barbecue is designed for those outdoor moments when cooking and eating alfresco make outdoor entertaining a way of life. This structure not only features a cooking surface, but also has ample space for preparation and a spacious under-counter area for storing firewood. Attractive and compact, it is suitable for both garden and patio and will suit almost any garden style.

YOU WILL NEED

TOOLS

- shovel and/or spade
- tape measure
- carpenter's level
- straight-edged piece of wood
- builder's square
- trowel
- tamper (or pole)

MATERIALS

- concrete: 110lbs (50kg) cement; 440lbs (200kg) sand; 440lbs (200kg) crushed stone
- bricks: 270 facebricks; 58 paving bricks
- mortar: 165lbs (75kg) cement; 660lbs (300kg) sand; 62lbs (28kg) lime or plasticizer (optional)
- fill: 10½ cubic ft (0.3m³)
- sand (to bed pavers): 110lbs (50kg)
- metal grid: 36¼in x 18in (920mm x 450mm)
- form board: 9 cubic ft (0.25m²) rigid material (marine plywood)

2 WEEKENDS

OUTDOOR DINING

Built from low-maintenance facebrick, this functional and attractive barbecue requires basic bricklaying skills along with a little ingenuity. Matching paving bricks are used in the fire bed to form an exposed working surface. They are also used to finish the inside of the storage area.

The materials specified here do not allow for wastage or breakage, so more should be ordered. Instead of form board, a concrete slab could be cast to form the working surface.

TIPS Never use a precast concrete slab for the cooking surface of a barbecue unit unless you top it with fire-resistant clay brick pavers. Concrete will not withstand the high temperatures of an open fire and will invariably crack.

Try to work neatly, scraping excess mortar off the bricks as you build the courses. When you are working with facebricks in particular, it is easier to clean as you go instead of trying to scrub off dry mortar later.

1 Start by measuring and marking out an area 5¼ft x 31½in (1.6m x 800mm) with chalk or lime. Dig trenches 8in (200mm) wide and 6in (150mm) deep to accommodate strip foundations around the edges of the marked area. A slab foundation need only be approximately 4in (100mm) deep.

2 Mix concrete in the ratio 1:4:4 (cement:sand:stone), adding just enough water to make the mixture pliable and easy to use. To prevent the water being drawn out of the concrete, moisten the soil before placing the mixture in the trench. Compact the concrete thoroughly with a trowel or straight-edged plank, and leave to set overnight.

3 Loosely lay the bricks on the foundation as a guide to the finished position of the bench and mark out their position on the concrete with chalk or a carpenter's pencil.

4 Mix mortar and start laying the first course of bricks. Begin at one of the corners and use a carpenter's level to ensure that the first brick is absolutely level.

5 The structure will not be level and square — and you will not be able to fit the lid properly — unless your first course of bricks is laid correctly. Use a builder's square to check the accuracy of the corners and set the carpenter's level at various angles along the tops of the bricks to check levels throughout the building process.

6 Continue checking the accuracy of the brickwork with the carpenter's level and use the handle of the trowel to knock bricks into the correct position. If building against an existing structure, do not assume that it is square and level; rather rely on the accuracy of your own brickwork.

7 As the brickwork progresses, use the corner squares and string — or a pin and builder's line — to mark the level of each course. This will enable you to keep the wall level and all the courses perfectly horizontal. Remember that the string should line up with the upper surface of the course you are building.

8 Use a long carpenter's level from corner to corner to ensure that brickwork is progressing evenly. Check all courses in this way before stringing lines as described in Step 7.

9 Make the storage lid with the plywood and slats. Start by cutting five shallow channels across the width of the slats so that water does not collect on the lid.

10 Pre-drill the long slats and four cross-pieces before sandwiching the plywood between them. Screw the wood together and then attach the lid to the brickwork with hinges.

POTTING TABLE

EVERY GARDEN SHOULD have a corner where a plant lover can work, repotting seedlings and tending to cuttings. In the absence of a greenhouse or shelter of some kind, a permanent potting table can become the most utilitarian feature in the entire garden. Built from rustic rock-face brick and set against a solid wall, this potting table has been topped with a couple of sturdy, but attractive precast concrete stone slabs.

1 WEEKEND

YOU WILL NEED

TOOLS
- chalk, lime or flour
- tape measure
- shovel and/or spade
- straight-edge piece of wood
- carpenter's pencil
- carpenter's level
- builder's square
- trowel

MATERIALS
- concrete: 33lbs (15kg) cement; 132lbs (60kg) sand; 132lbs (60kg) stone
- mortar: 33lbs (15kg) cement; 132lbs (60kg) sand
- bricks: 64 facebricks
- precast concrete stone or concrete slabs: 2 slabs x 34½in x 8¼in x 1½in (880mm x 210mm x 40mm)

POTTERING AROUND

The piers (or pillars) that support the slab for this potting table are built with four bricks in each course, and stand slightly away from the adjacent wall. The materials that have been specified for this project allow for a solid foundation slab about 2in (50mm) thick. If the piers are built farther apart, you can throw two separate slabs.

If you are to use this table for potting plants, locate it adjacent to a wall either in the garden or against the house. Ideally, it should be sited away from prevailing winds and in a location that will get some shade. Ultimately, the size will be determined by the precast concrete stone or precast concrete slabs available in your area. If the dimensions of this table are too small for your own needs, adapt the measurements or even increase the number of supporting piers required and use larger – or more – slabs. You could even add extra piers to make the surface longer.

This table could also be situated in an entertaining area, where a solid surface is required for serving food and refreshments. Built on a slightly bigger scale, and perhaps finished with a timber top, it could even be utilized for alfresco meals. The same four-brick pier configuration is equally suitable for pillars designed to support sawn and planed timber for a pergola. Pillars would obviously be sited much farther apart; the only other major difference would be their height, and the fact that some sort of reinforcing would be required. Either galvanized-iron strapping would be set in the concrete footings; or, if the pillars are to be more substantial, you may need metal reinforcing rods.

1 Mark out an area approximately 3¼ft x 20in (1m x 500mm) and dig a trench for the foundation slab, which should be at least 2in (50mm) thick. Mix the concrete and place in the trench. With a straight-edged piece of wood, use a chopping action to compact and flatten the concrete and expel all air. Use the carpenter's level to check that it is level.

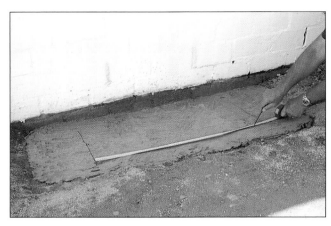

2 When the concrete has set, measure and mark the position of the two piers. This will guide you as you lay your first courses of brick. make sure they are positioned so that your two slabs can span them with a slight overlap at each end.

3 Mix the mortar in the ratio 1:4 (cement:sand), adding lime or plasticizer if you wish. Lay a ⅖–⅗in-thick (10–15mm) sausage of mortar on the concrete where the first brick is to be laid. Use the tip of the trowel to make a jagged furrow through the center of the mortar.

4 Place the first brick in the mortar, tapping gently with the trowel to make sure it is firmly bedded.

5 It is essential that the first course of bricks is absolutely level. Use the carpenter's level to check the horizontal surface periodically as you work and, if a brick is not level, remove it, scrape off the mortar with the trowel and start again.

6 When the first four bricks have been laid to form the first course, fill the central cavity with mortar and, if you wish, hardpan (or crushed stone). If hardpan is added to the mortar, this will create a strong, concrete-filled central core.

7 Now lay the first course of the second pier, using the square to check and make absolutely certain that the two piers are at right-angles to one another. Use the level across the two piers to ensure that the upper surface of all the bricks is straight and at the same level.

8 Continue building the two piers course by course, filling in the central core and checking across the top of the bricks as you progress. Do not forget to check the vertical planes of the brickwork too.

9 When both piers have been completed, cover the top of each with a layer of mortar about ⅜in (10mm) thick, smoothing it out evenly with the trowel.

10 Place the two slabs over the pillars so that they overlap evenly on all sides. Check the upper surface with the level to ensure that it is indeed level. If it is not absolutely level, either remove or add a little of the mortar beneath one side of the slab to rectify.

BRICK-PAVED PATH

BRICK PAVING MAY be as rustic or formal as you wish. The secret is largely in the line it follows. Laid in a straight, regular way, paving will add formality; laid along a windy track, with plants cascading over its edges, a brick path can introduce a charm and mystery that belies the material from which it is constructed. This quaint path meanders for nearly 33ft (10m), beckoning those who walk along it to continue towards a promising leafy glade.

2 WEEKENDS

YOU WILL NEED

TOOLS

- shovel and/or spade
- carpenter's level
- rubber mallet
- broom

MATERIALS

- paving bricks: 252 for the path; 84 for the edging (one side only)
- sand: 1105lbs (500kg)
- cement: 44lbs (20kg) (optional)

A WINDING WALKWAY

No specialist tools or bricklaying skills are required to lay this brick path. It is, however, essential that the bricks are laid on a well-compacted surface and that they are laid level. Provided the surface is stable, the bricks may be laid on a thick bed of sand without mortar. Sand, or a weak mixture of sand and cement is then brushed over the surface to aid bonding. An edging will keep the bricks in place; this project utilizes bricks set into the soil alongside the paving on one side, where the ground slopes. The other side is effectively held in place by soil and plants.

If laid across an open lawn, edge both sides of the path. Alternatively, lay bricks flat – in mortar – along the edge of the path to prevent the paving from moving.

A simple basketweave has been used here, but a running bond (*see page 114*) would work equally well.

TIP The path should slope very slightly across its width. If built into a slope (as it is here), ensure that the fall is towards the bank and not away from it.

1 If the path is to be built in an open area of the garden, peg it out with string, marking the line you want it to follow. This path is 33ft (10m) long and about 26in (660mm) wide (excluding the edging). Remove all vegetation and stones and then compact well.

2 Lay a bed of sand 1¼–2in (30–50mm) thick along the first three feet to be paved. Use a long carpenter's level (or a long straight-edged length of timber with a carpenter's level on top of it) to scrape the sand flat and ensure that it is level.

3 Lay a header course of bricks at one end of the path, abutting them tightly up against each other. Tap the bricks gently with the rubber mallet to make sure that they are well bedded in the sand. Use a carpenter's level to check.

4 Start laying the basketweave pattern, alternating the direction in which each pair of bricks is laid. Again, tap gently with the rubber mallet to make sure that they are level. Use a carpenter's level to check that the horizontal plane is flat. If it not, tap a little more with the mallet until it is.

5 If the path curves, there will be slightly wider gaps between the bricks on the outer curve. You can either use mortar at these points, or, if you plan to plant between the bricks, fill in with good-quality soil.

6 Once you have laid the first ten feet of the path, sweep sand (or a sand-and-cement mixture no stronger than 1:4 cement:sand) over the surface.

7 Before you continue with the next stretch of path, place the edging. This will prevent any possibility of the outside bricks dislodging when you walk over them. Gently dig a trench 6in (150mm) deep alongside the path and place the bricks side by side in the trench, as if in a sailor course (*see page 119*).

8 Fill in with soil on the other side of the path so that the upper surface of the bricks is no higher than the surrounding soil. Water gently with a hose to help the soil settle. Once the soil has settled, you can plant alongside the path and fill with soil any gaps that may still remain between the bricks.

GARDEN STEPS

AN ATTRACTIVE FLIGHT of low steps leads up a grass bank in an expansive country garden, neatening a previously trampled slope. The same neat design would be equally at home in a small townhouse garden or used for steps leading to a patio. Although brick has been used to build these garden steps, the treads are precast concrete stone pavers, which contrast both in color and texture to the red-hued brick. Maintaining the mixed-media theme, these steps lead from a simple pathway created with brick and compacted gravel.

1 WEEKEND

YOU WILL NEED

TOOLS
- pegs and string or line
- straight-edge and/or carpenter's level
- shovel and/or spade
- trowel
- stonemason's hammer or tamper

MATERIALS
- concrete: 88lbs (40kg) premix
- bricks: 32 facebricks
- precast concrete stone slabs: 12 slabs x 8¼in x 8¼in (210mm x 210mm)
- mortar: 88lbs (40kg) premix
- crushed stone: 110lbs (50kg)
- sand: 55lbs (25kg)

TIPS When building steps into a slope, start from the bottom and work upwards. This will enable you to bond each tread with the one below.

STEPPING UP

This is a reasonably simple project, which should not take more than a day or two to complete. The bricks are laid on a concrete foundation with mortar to bind them, and unless your slope is considerably steeper than this one, you will not have to build walls as each riser is only a single brick-high wall. Precast concrete paving blocks are used for the treads – for variety and interest more than anything else; for a more formal effect, use bricks throughout.

Before you start building, you will need to check the overall rise of the slope in your garden. You can do this by building a simple profile with two lengths of wood nailed together – one long enough to cover the length of the steps and the other to fit the total depth. The ends of the timber are nailed at a 90-degree angle where they meet. If, for instance, the total length of the steps is 4ft (1.2m) and the depth 23½in (600mm), simple mathematics will indicate that you can build three steps 15¾in (400mm) deep with risers measuring 8in (200mm).

The gradual slope tackled in this project allows for an easy stairway of four 35½in-wide (900mm) and 3in-high (80mm) steps, each with a 14in-deep (360mm) tread. Ordinary facebricks are used throughout; if bricks are to be used instead of paving slabs, add six bricks for every tread. Since only a minimal amount of concrete and mortar is required for the project, it is sensible to use premixed packs. If you have cement and sand on hand, mix 22lbs (10kg) of cement with 66lbs (30kg) of soft sand for the mortar. For the concrete, you need about the same amount of cement and sand, plus 66lbs (30kg) of stone.

1 Having decided where the steps will begin and end, you need to work out how many steps will fit the slope and peg them out. Start by pegging out the two bottom steps and then use a long carpenter's level – or a straight-edged length of timber with a carpenter's level on top of it – to ascertain the upper level of the second step. The distance between each peg is 14in (360mm) – the depth of a tread – and the height from the upper level measured here is 6¼in (160mm).

2 Once you have checked that the pegs are in the correct position, and that all the corners are at 90 degrees, cut into the bank and excavate a trench to accommodate the bottom step. The deepest part of the trench will be at the back and this should be about 6in (150mm) deep. The front of the trench will only be about 3in (75mm) deep. Note that these measurements will vary according to the slope in your own garden. Increase the dimensions if necessary.

3 Make sure that the earth is well compacted at the base of the trench before you start laying the steps. Mix the mortar and lay two bricks on each side and three in front, regularly checking the levels.

4 Fill the trench with a 2⅓in (60mm) layer of crushed stone and compact the surface well with the top of the club hammer or with a tamper. This will aid drainage.

5 Cover the stone with building sand, allowing it to fill any gaps that may remain in the hardpan layer. Compact thoroughly before placing the slabs on top.

6 Once you are sure that the slabs are absolutely level with the brickwork, lay mortar over the stones at the back of the trench, compacting and levelling well.

7 Before you fill the joints with mortar, lay the front row of bricks that will form the riser for the second step. Fill all the joints between the bricks and the slabs with mortar, chopping it in carefully with the trowel. Wipe away any excess mortar to avoid staining.

8 Excavate behind the first step and repeat Steps 3 to 7. Once the second step has been built, excavate for the third step and repeat the process until all four steps have been built. Lay a final course of four bricks at the back of the top step, as in Step 7.

TRADITIONAL SUNDIAL

USED SINCE AT least 1500BC, and wildly popular during the 16th century, the sundial is used for marking time according to the position of the shadow cast by the sun. Often positioned as a central feature or focal point in the garden, sundials may be mounted on many different bases and pillars which, imaginatively constructed, can become features on their own. This simple brick base and pier support a precast slab onto which a beautifully crafted sundial has been set.

1 WEEKEND

YOU WILL NEED

TOOLS

- chalk
- shovel and/or spade
- tape measure
- carpenter's level
- builder's square
- trowel

MATERIALS

- concrete: 22lbs (10kg) cement; 88lbs (40kg) sand; 88lbs (40kg) stone
- bricks: 31 facebricks
- mortar: 44lbs (20kg) premixed cement and sand
- precast concrete stone slab: 18½in x 22½in (470mm x 570mm)
- brass sundial
- epoxy

TIME WILL TELL

There are many types of sundials, but the most common is the horizontal dial, made with a flat, usually circular brass or bronze plate with a triangular gnomon — the fixed object whose shadow will serve as the indicator to show the time. Having sourced an instrument, the next step is to decide which type of pedestal you will set it on. While precast concrete and stone are common choices, brick provides a remarkably versatile option, since the size of the pedestal can be easily adapted to suit the size of the dial itself. This simple 27½in-high (700mm) brick structure was designed and built to support a round brass sundial with a diameter of 10in (250mm). The dial is epoxied to the center of a precast concrete stone slab.

The pedestal is built on a relatively small foundation slab, which is first paved with seven ordinary facebricks. The pier of the pedestal is built with three bricks per course — a configuration that would also be suitable to support a pergola roof, provided it is reinforced with strapping. Although a slightly rectangular slab has been used to top the pedestal, a larger square slab would also be appropriate. Since little mortar is used, premixed material is recommended.

TIP First find a suitable sundial. If it is bigger than the one used here, you may need a larger slab for the top of the pedestal, in which case the piers should be built with four bricks per course.

1 Lay the seven bricks for the base on the ground and mark around them using chalk or flour about 4in (100mm) away from the edge of the bricks. Remove the bricks and dig a trench 2–4in (50–100mm) deep. Compact the soil in the base of the trench before mixing the concrete in a wheelbarrow or on a clean, dry surface using just enough water to make the mixture pliable. Place the concrete in the trench, level and compact, and allow to set, preferably overnight.

2 Once the concrete has set, lay the first brick on a sausage of mortar. Tap firmly into place with the handle of the trowel and use the level to make sure that it is level. The three bricks in the center will form the first course of the pier, while those on the outside will create the effect of a brick base. Make sure every single brick is level and square.

3 Build up the pier using stretcher bond (*see page 114*), so that each brick overlaps two beneath it.

4 Clean all surfaces of the brickwork as you work to prevent staining and use the carpenter's level on both horizontal and vertical surfaces.

5 Once all eight courses have been completed, place a little mortar on the upper surface and place the slab on top. Push it gently into the mortar and check once again with the level that it is straight and level.

6 Before you attach the sundial to the slab, be sure to position it correctly by following the manufacturer's instructions. Once the brass dial is in place and shows the time accurately, use epoxy to fit it to the slab.

SCREEN WALL

DESIGNED TO SCREEN a garden patio from the garage attached to a suburban house, this facebrick wall, built using a straightforward stretcher bond, doubles as the back of a simple wooden bench. Since the finish of the bricks is quite coarse, timber slats have been screwed to the brickwork to create a back rest. A planter built at one end adds character, not only breaking the straight line of the brickwork, but enabling you to add color with shrubs and flowers.

YOU WILL NEED

TOOLS

- tape measure
- builder's square
- pegs or nails and builder's line or string
- chalk or hydrated lime
- shovel and/or spade
- several straight-edged lengths of wood, long and short
- carpenter's level
- mason's trowel
- corner blocks and builder's line
- pointing/jointing tool

MATERIALS

- concrete: 155lbs (70kg) cement; 620lbs (280kg) sand; 620lbs (280kg) stone
- bricks: 480 facebricks
- mortar: 330lbs (150kg) cement; 1325lbs (600kg) sand; 165lbs (75kg) lime, or plasticizer (optional)

3–4 WEEKENDS

OFF THE WALL

You will need to allow a series of weekends to complete this project, which is both time consuming and exacting, rather than difficult. It should not, however, be attempted without some skilled assistance unless you have already completed other brick projects and are confident that you can maintain the plumb of a wall of this height.

The materials specified will enable you to build a 6ft-high (1.8m), 11½ft-long (3.5m) wall in facebrick with three supporting pillars behind the wall.

If you opt to include seating, an additional 60 bricks will be needed for the lower piers supporting the timber. You will need 12 x 6ft x 2¾in-wide (1.8m x 70mm) slats for the seat, each set of six forming half the bench, joining at the center of the middle pier. The wood that forms the back rest should be at least 8¼–10ft (2.5–3m) long.

Foundations for a wall this height are more substantial than for other projects. Although a 1:4:4 concrete mix is specified, if soil conditions are at all unstable, use a stronger 1:3:6 mix, or seek professional advice.

1 Set out the foundation trenches using a retractable steel tape and a builder's square for accuracy. Make sure that the trenches are 4in (100mm) wider on all sides than the structure itself. Peg out the area using long nails or pegs and string, incorporating 13⅓in x 13⅓in (340mm x 340mm) pillars in the center and one at each end.

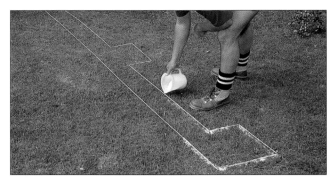

2 To make digging easier, mark along the line of the string with lime, chalk or even flour.

3 Remove grass sods carefully and dig to a depth of 8–10in (200–250mm). Keep the bottom of the foundation trench as even and level as possible to enable you to cast an even slab.

4 Once you have dug the trench, place bricks at intervals along the trench and then set a long straight edge across the bricks, with a carpenter's level on top of it to ensure the trench is indeed level.

5 Place the concrete in the trench and then compact with the short straight edge of the spade, using a chopping movement to expel any air bubbles. If you are including piers for built-in seating, throw the foundations for these at the same time. Allow the concrete to set thoroughly overnight.

6 Before you mix the mortar to lay the bricks, loosely lay the first course on the foundation – do not use mortar – to check the layout of the wall. Now is the time to rectify any mistakes.

7 If you are building piers for seating, these should be built opposite the supporting pillars on the outside of the wall.

8 Start building the wall at the first pillar, which comprises four bricks, so that it will bond with the single brick wall. Lay the bricks on mortar and check across all angles to ensure they are flat and level.

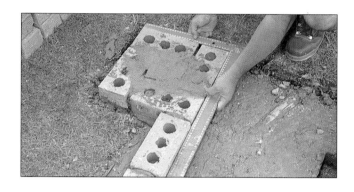

9 Fill the center of the pillar with mortar or concrete; alternatively, fill in with half a brick. As you continue with the length of wall, use the builder's square to check that the brickwork is, in fact, square.

10 Working in a stretcher bond (*see page 114*), continue to build the wall to the required height. A total of 20 courses will result in a height of about 6ft (1.8m) if the patio is brick paved once the wall is complete. Use corner blocks and string — or a pin and line — to keep the brickwork absolutely straight.

11 Build the pillars up to the same height as the wall, using the carpenter's level to check the vertical surface as well as the horizontal surface as you work. Use the pointing tool to neaten joints as you progress.

12 If you are including the bench, screw the wood to the piers (for the seat) and to the wall (for the back rest).

157

WOOD

ONE OF THE MOST versatile materials for garden structures and decorative outdoor features, wood can be used in a myriad of styles to suit any garden design. Easily accessible and available in many forms — including poles, logs, rustic beams, laths and smooth-cut timber — it offers a wealth of possibilities in terms of construction, from the simplest log step pathway to the most elaborate garden building. Even if other materials (brick or stone, for instance) are the primary construction material in your garden, wood may be used to introduce another, very appealing element.

Features and structures built from wood range from the highly decorative to simply rustic and strictly practical, depending on your needs and, of course, your carpentry skills. The options are equally vast and varied: from straightforward garden fences to pergolas, wooden decks and challenging arches, walkways and open lattice-work screens. It is also a popular material for building the more conventional seats, tables and other garden furniture. Since working with wood is usually less labor intensive than bricks, stone or concrete, this material is a particularly popular option for DIY enthusiasts.

There is also great scope for wood in the garden. A novice can simply place a single railway tie on loose blocks to create an instant bench, while those with some carpentry skills will probably want to tackle a more challenging project that may involve latticework or wooden cut-outs. A rustic garden bench (*see pages 184–187*) may be erected in just a few hours, while a wooden cabin clad with factory-machined tongue-and-groove slats will take time, effort and specialized tools to complete.

The projects featured here cater for all tastes and range from a simple but highly effective screen made with round, rustic laths, to a planed-wood arbor, painted white in contrast to the natural wood around it. For interest and variety, different wood types have been used throughout and, in most instances, these may be easily altered to change the look while utilizing the same basic design.

IDEAS & INSPIRATION

Wood has been used to build garden buildings, outdoor structures and decorative garden features for centuries. Age-old arbors were found in ancient Egypt and trellised pergolas were common in Rome, the classic colonnaded structures later imitated by Italian garden designers of the Renaissance. Elaborate wooden galleries and walkways became common in Europe from the 13th century and were highly popular in colonial America, while garden arbors remain popular in Mediterranean countries.

Fences as features

Open-board fencing, popular in 16th-century China, came into its own in England a couple of centuries later when landscape gardeners copied the Chinese designs.

Today, open-board fences are practical rather than pretty. Picket-like fencing built by early settlers in America often comprised simple boards sharpened at one end so they could be easily knocked into the ground. They were then held together by a single rail at the top. As new towns sprung up in the colonial era in America, Australia and South Africa, both post-and-rail and picket fences became commonplace. As a result, today's fence designs tend to vary from place to place. In New England, which is world renowned for its colonial American picket fencing, the designs are elegant, while those fences inspired by Victorian England are rather fanciful, with ornamental posts and patterns cut out of the pickets.

All hands on deck

Wooden decks evolved from porches that were extensions of the house and from Japanese platforms, which were either freestanding or built against the house. Although the original version was designed as a viewing deck, modern designs provide an opportunity for outdoor living.

BELOW *In this delightfully informal garden, a rustic timber fence is ingeniously built between stone pillars.*

Garden retreats

Ever since the Romans built their extravagant retreats away from their villas and palaces, traditional pavilions, gazebos and other more modest retreats have become well within the realms of DIY builders. Garden books and magazines are a constant source of inspiration. Victorian designs are wonderfully inventive, and range from neat structures to fabulous rustic work.

Much the same is true of other elements of the traditional garden, such as bridges. Since water has always been essential to Chinese and Japanese Zen gardens, bridges are common in gardens of these genres, and many are still built with the pavilion-type roof that has become popular in English and European gardens. Less frivolous than many of the English styles, wooden bridges built in 19th-century America also borrowed ideas from the Chinese and European designs.

Outdoor living

When it comes to making wooden garden furniture, the rustic style does not involve difficult joints and sophisticated carpentry, but the results are charming. Designs date back to the 1700s, when rather elegant rustic furniture became popular. Latter-day furniture is, however, less refined.

Read books and visit public gardens. Drive through suburbs where you can catch a glimpse of other people's ideas. If necessary, summon up the courage and ask if you can take a closer look. More often than not people are flattered when others want to copy what they have.

Even though most wooden structures blend well with just about any garden, make sure your chosen design does indeed suit your property before you buy materials.

ABOVE *Planed wood and relatively simple latticework lend this gazebo a sophisticated air.*
BELOW *This attractive wooden structure can serve to bridge both man-made and natural water courses in a garden.*

TOOLS, TIPS & TECHNIQUES

You do not have to be a master craftsman to build a garden structure out of wood, although some carpentry skills will be necessary for certain projects. It is important, however, to have the correct tools for the job. While the simplest structures may be erected with only a hammer and nails – or may even be wired together – more refined designs will require proper joints, screws and bolts. To build anything that looks professional and will last, it is also essential to master certain basic construction techniques and to utilize materials suitable for the particular structure.

TOOLS

Most regular do-it-yourselfers already have the essential tools required for all the projects featured here. Power tools make the job easier, especially when it comes to cutting wood, but if you do not have these, consider renting them.

Basic items

A **wheelbarrow** is useful when it comes to moving materials and for mixing small quantities of concrete required for foundation footings. A gardener's wheelbarrow is too shallow; you will need a standard builder's wheelbarrow.

A **spade** is essential for digging foundation footings where these are required, and a **shovel** may be used for mixing and moving the foundation concrete. An **auger** or **post-hole borer** is handy for drilling holes for upright posts. Since the hole is straight-sided and much smaller than any hole you can dig with a spade, the post fits neatly and seldom needs to be set in concrete. A large **garden fork** and a **rake** are also useful tools. If excavating hard or stony ground, you will probably also need a **pick**. For compaction around poles, another pole is usually quite adequate for small jobs. Alternatively, make a tamper or tamping tool by filling an empty one-gallon can with concrete and setting a broomstick-sized pole inside it. You can also attach a hefty block of wood to the end of a sturdy stick, but the concrete/can combination works best.

Whatever you are making, wood needs to be measured and structures will need to be correctly laid out, so a good-quality retractable **tape measure** is indispensable.

If you are building a treehouse or any other garden building that has some sort of beam or roof structure, a **ladder** will also be a prerequisite. And, since most timber is either oiled, varnished or painted, clean **paint brushes** should always be in your basic toolkit.

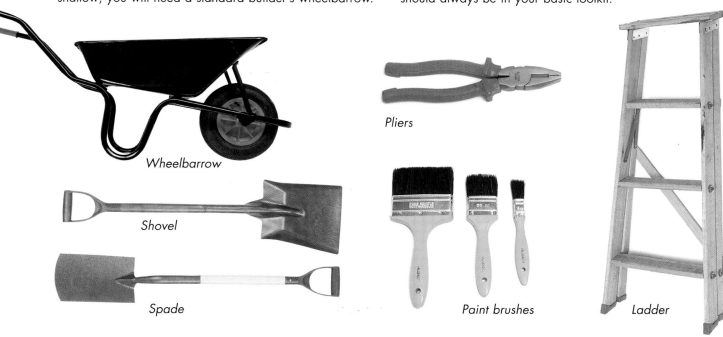

Wheelbarrow

Shovel

Spade

Pliers

Paint brushes

Ladder

Finally, make sure you have **pliers** handy in case you need to pull out unwanted nails. These may also be used to cut wire.

Laying out

Apart from furniture, wooden structures will need to be laid out before work begins. **Lime, chalk, cement** or even **flour** may be used for the smaller structures, but **pegs** and some sort of **line** are more suitable for larger buildings as well as pergolas, walkways and so on. **Metal pegs** are usually sold with **builder's line**, or you can make small wooden stakes and use them with household string. A **stonemason's hammer** is useful for knocking pegs and stakes into the ground.

Unless you are building an octagonal or hexagonal gazebo, you will need to ensure that all corners are square, and a **metal builder's square** is thus essential. To double-check that the layout is square, use the 3:4:5 method. Measure and mark 10ft (3m), depending on the size of the structure) from the corner; then measure and mark 13ft (4m) to create a right angle. If the corner is indeed square, the distance between the two marks will be 16ft (5m). This technique may also be used to check various other square elements of the building process.

Levels

No project, no matter how simple it may appear to be, should be tackled without a **carpenter's level**. This will help you keep a check on accuracy, and is usually available in a variety of lengths, with both a horizontal and a vertical indicator for checking surfaces as you work. A **carpenter's square**, which will also prove indispensable, incorporates a small spirit vial and can be used to check that planes are both square and level.

Another useful item is a homemade **water level**, which may be made from transparent tubing (or a length of garden hose with transparent tubing inserted into each end). Invaluable when working on a slope in the garden or when establishing the correct height of poles and posts for pergolas and other garden buildings, it works on the basic principle that water finds its own level. The tubing is filled with water and one end is affixed to one of the posts in the ground so that the water level aligns with the top of the pole. The other end is then held against a second post to check that it is the same height.

A **carpenter's pencil** (or, in fact, any other lead pencil) will be needed for marking the position of the water level or beams, struts, crosspieces and so on.

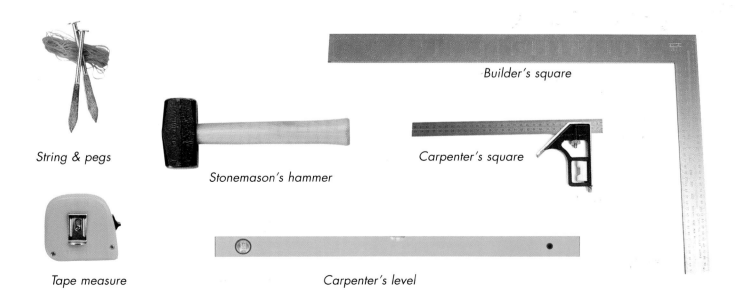

String & pegs

Stonemason's hammer

Builder's square

Carpenter's square

Tape measure

Carpenter's level

Carpentry

Whichever type of wood you choose to use (*see pages 165–166*), you will need cutting tools as well as **hammers, screwdrivers** and **wrenches** to connect various components. Although you can, if you wish, buy most of the wood already cut to size, you will still need a saw of some description to trim ends and cut accurate angles for joints, no matter how basic. **Power saws** make light work of much of the cutting process as they cut more quickly and smoothly than handsaws – although it is not always easy to be absolutely accurate.

Only the very basic items for the various projects are specified here. If you find you enjoy working with wood, you may decide to add to your carpentry toolkit at a later stage.

Generally, a **circular saw** is used to cut in a straight line at any angle, while a general-purpose **jigsaw** has a multitude of uses, and is invaluable when you need to make more intricate cuts and curves. If you are going to

be cutting poles, posts and planks to size, consider buying your own circular saw. There are various types available, from smaller hand-held models to those manufactured for mounting on a worktable for use as a **bench saw**. The latter may be used for bevelled cuts and is favored by earnest woodworkers.

The most useful handsaws include **tenon saws**, which are invaluable for fine and intricate work, and general-purpose **hacksaws**. A **crosscut saw**, or even a smaller **panel saw**, is useful for slicing the ends of posts, battens and so on, while a **bow saw** comes into its own when you need to cut logs and poles. **Ripsaws** are designed for cutting along the grain of the wood.

Planes, rasps and **files**, although not specified as necessary tools in any of the following projects, are useful for shaping and finishing wood. **Chisels** are ideal for cutting notches and for trimming edges neatly. An **angle grinder** is the ideal tool for cutting railway ties and other

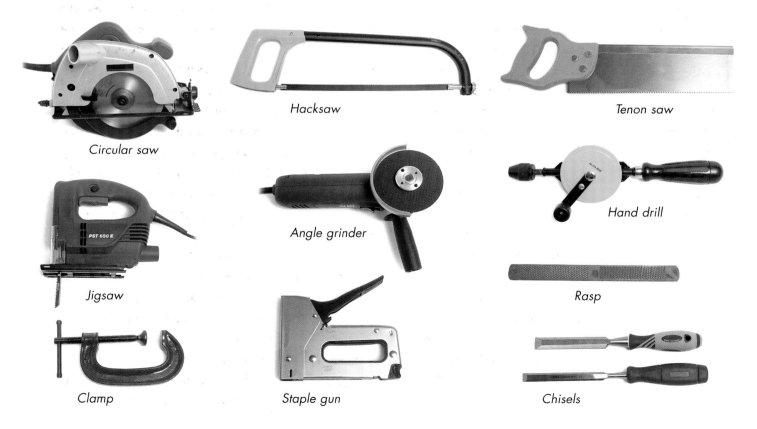

Circular saw

Hacksaw

Tenon saw

Jigsaw

Angle grinder

Hand drill

Rasp

Clamp

Staple gun

Chisels

really hard woods, and it may also be used for smoothing the edges of poles – although you could also use a **belt sande**r, which is the recommended tool for smoothing planks and boards.

Finally, even though any flat, secure working surface will enable you to complete all the projects detailed here, a solid **workbench** will make the tasks easier. Portable workbenches with built-in clamps are ideal for working outdoors. These may also be folded flat and stored out of the way when not in use. When working on a tight budget, inexpensive **trestles** are a common choice.

When it comes to fixing and fastening the wood, one tool you cannot be without is an ordinary **claw hammer**. This is used for driving nails in, as well as for extracting bent or incorrectly angled nails. A smaller **tack hammer** is easier to use when knocking short nails and tacks into small-scale items. To tighten bolts and coach screws, you will also need **screwdrivers** and **wrenches**. Ideally, buy a good-quality set of wrenches and invest in a ratchet screw-driver with the full range of screw heads.

Clamps are useful to hold pieces of wood firmly together when gluing, cutting and nailing, but are not essential.

You will also need a **drill** of some sort to make holes in the wood for screws, nails and decorative features (*see page 178, step 5*). A heavy-duty **bit brace** or a **hand drill** should suffice if you are only likely to be drilling a few holes; otherwise, invest in a **power drill**, which may also be used to speed up the task of tightening screws. You will of course need a selection of **drill bits** for an electric drill, including a range of different-sized flat wood drill bits, which will enable you to make holes for a selection of bolts and screws.

A **nail gun** is a wonderful tool, but they are quite expensive and unless you plan to do a great deal of woodwork, probably not worth the investment. A **staple gun** may be cheaper, but only useful for fastening shadecloth, canvas and other suitable outdoor fabrics to structures, or for joining reasonably thin trelliswork.

MATERIALS & CONSTRUCTION METHODS

There is a wide choice of timber and construction methods when it comes to building structures in the garden. Suitable timber ranges from sawn and possibly planed hardwoods and softwoods to rustic poles and sliced logs, which may still have its bark. In addition, where posts and poles are set in foundations, you will need concrete,. If the structure is to be roofed or covered in some way, you will require some kind of roof sheeting or shadecloth. You will also need the nails, screws and bolts to fasten components.

Wood

The type of wood chosen for garden projects will depend largely on what is available. A wide range of trees is felled commercially, but not all species grow in every country. Generally, the choice is between hardwoods and softwoods; some types are better suited to poles, others to planks, battens, boards and so on. Hardwoods include mahogany, oak, ash, elm, cherry and meranti. Meranti is a good choice for building decks. However, many people limit their use of hardwoods to outdoor furniture. Even though the term 'hardwood' refers to the botanical decid-uous classification of the trees, they are indeed tough and difficult to cut. Generally less costly than the hardwoods, and easier to saw and plane, softwoods are cut from coniferous trees, including pine and redwood. Ironically, while redwood (which grows very slowly) is renowned for its durability and resistance to decay, wood from some quick-growing pines requires frequent maintenance if it is to last outdoors.

- **Poles** – for pergolas, rustic shelters, decks, bridges and fences – are relatively inexpensive, easy to handle and are often used for the quick erection of structures. There is usually a choice between rustic poles that have simply been debarked, and those that have been machined to a smooth surface to make them reasonably regular in size. Split poles, useful for railings and screen structures, are also available commercially.

Whatever type is to be used, choose poles pretreated against infestation and rot. Traditionally, hardwood poles were coated with creosote, a dark-brown oil distilled from coal tar, to preserve them. Creosote is, however, toxic to plants and causes materials such as shadecloth to rot. It is now more common for sawmills to impregnate poles with substances such as water-based chromated copper arsenate (CCA), which gives them a green tinge. If untreated poles are to be anchored in the ground, the bottoms should be coated with a bituminous waterproofing compound or with creosote, or they are likely to deteriorate rapidly underground. Since bitumen, which is derived from petroleum, is available in a non-toxic, water-soluble form, this has become the more popular choice, particular for DIY use.

■ **Laths** may be sawn or rustic. The sawn version, split into thin strips, is suitable for trellises or latticework. Round laths are rustic in appearance, and are grown rather than manufactured – fashioned from straight saplings (wattle, for example) and neither machined nor treated. While this lack of preparation prior to selling round laths may limit their lifespan, it means that they are inexpensive. The rustic version is ideal for screens and fences, and even for garden seating (*see pages 184–187*) and unsophisticated pergola roofs.

The greener the wood, the easier it will be to work with; as they dry, laths tend to split, so pre-drill holes and use screws rather than nails to secure them.

■ **Sawn lumber**, which is sold commercially for construction, is cut to form planks, beams, battens and posts. It is available rough-sawn, planed all round (PAR) or dressed all round (DAR). DAR is the most expensive option and PAR the standard choice for garden structures.

■ **Waney board** has an uneven edge and some bark on one side, while 'rustic' timber has all its bark on one side. This is essentially the first cut from the log. Usually scrapped or sold cheaply, it is untreated and suitable for siding structures required for short-term use.

Bark-clad timber is thicker, more uniform and is usually treated. While more expensive, it has a similar visual effect and lasts longer.

■ **Railway ties** may be used for outdoor structures. Made from tough hardwoods, they are ideal for steps, planters and even for edging small patios. Used with other hard materials and plants, they also make rather attractive pathways. Since ties are now being made from concrete, the old timber type is becoming more and more scarce.

Laths

Poles

Sawn lumber

Remember that, for safety reasons, structural timber must be pre-treated. Dimensions must be compatible with the scale of the structure. Timber supporting the pales of a picket fence would not suit decking. When choosing roof timber, remember that the covering will determine the dimensions of beams that support the roof sheeting.

Timber merchants use nominal sizes when describing timber; these relate to the original dimensions of the wood and do not take wastage into account. Sizes specified in the following projects are guidelines; if these are not available, choose something similar.

Foundations and footings

Where foundations are required for buildings, or footings for poles and posts, you will need cement, sand and stone, mixed together with water in the required ratio.

Ordinary Portland cement may be used for almost all DIY projects. Sold in sealed paper sacks, cement hardens when it is mixed with water and gains its strength over a period of time as it dries out and 'cures'. It should be stored in a dry place, and discarded if the dry cement becomes hard or lumpy. The sand mixed with the cement must be clean and fairly coarse or 'sharp'. River sand is usually suitable, but it should be graded, so buy it from a reputable supplier. Do not be tempted to use unwashed beach or dune sand.

The crushed stone used to make concrete is available in various sizes, but for small building projects, a ¾in (19–20mm) aggregate is ideal.

The properties of concrete depend on the proportions of cement, sand, stone and water used in the mixture. Low-strength concrete is perfectly adequate for most garden projects, so combine the dry materials 1:4:4 (cement:sand:stone) with just enough water to produce a workable mix. For pillars and posts that are to support a roof structure (a pergola or carport, for instance), a stronger 1:3:4 mix is advised.

Construction

Measure the wood two or three times before cutting and check the lengths of screws and nails before you start.

Although the angle used to work different saws varies slightly (for instance, a flatter position is used with a tenon saw), the movement is the same. Whether you are using a power tool or handsaw, never force the blade through the wood. For accuracy, clamp the wood to a workbench.

When it comes to fixing and fastening wood, drill holes in the right place, using the correct drill bit. If you are pre-drilling pilot holes for nails and screws, use a twist bit; for screws with countersunk heads, you need a countersink bit; for other holes, the selection of flat wood bits must match the size of your screws and bolts. All pilot holes should be shorter and narrower than your nail or screw.

Most of the projects featured here rely on simple joints: many are nailed together with ordinary butt joints, some of which are mitered. Complicated gazebo and pergola designs may call for halving joints, where lengths of timber are partially cut away or notched so they slot together.

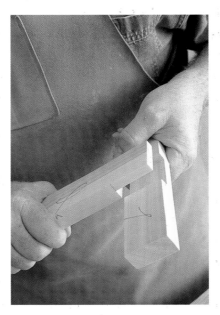

Halving joint

LOG STEPS

THE SIMPLE COMBINATION of a rustic stairway made with round poles and a stepping-stone path created with slices of a pine tree trunk is both inexpensive and easy to do. Perfect for a slight slope in an informal garden, it has expansive treads that may either be planted or filled with compacted gravel. As a feature, this step-and-path combo adds form to the garden and may be used to link different areas with different functions.

1 WEEKEND

YOU WILL NEED

TOOLS

- shovel and/or spade
- tape measure
- stonemason's hammer and pegs
- carpenter's level
- hammer
- chalk

MATERIALS

- logs: 8 poles x 6ft x 4in (1.8m x 100mm)
- split poles: 8 poles x 20in x 4in (500mm x 100mm)
- stepping stones: 5 or more wood slices, with 1½–1¾in (40–45mm) diameter
- sand: 44lbs (20kg) builder's sand
- split poles for sides: 6 poles x 3½ft x 4in (1.1m x 100mm); 6 poles x 21½in x 4in (550mm x 100mm) (optional)
- wire nails: 12 nails x 4in (100mm) (optional)
- soil: for fill (if required)

A STEP AHEAD

Either logs or round poles may be used to build a stairway into a bank or on a gentle slope in the garden. The slope will determine not only how many treads to build, but also the exact dimensions of both these and the width of the steps. Before you start, you will need to measure the slope and, with the aid of a simple profile, establish how many steps you will need to build. The steps here were built into a slope no higher than 27½in (700mm). By measuring 10ft (3m) from the top of the bank to the start of the first tread, three 3¼ft-deep (1m) steps are accommodated. For the profile, nail two lengths (27½in and 10ft/700mm and 3m) of wood together at right angles and position the longer piece at the point of the uppermost step. If yours is a steeper slope, you will probably need to cut into the bank and retain the soil at either side of the stairway, perhaps with a rock garden (*see page 24*).

TIP If you have a chain saw and a suitable log, you can cut your own wood slices. Purchasing them from a nursery or sawmill means that they are often treated with a preservative that will help prevent them from deteriorating too rapidly and eventually rotting away.

1 Once you have decided where to build the steps and have established how many will fit the slope, peg out the position of the first riser, knocking two pegs into the ground 6ft (1.8m) apart. Mark a square the width of your spade, approximately 8in x 8in (200mm x 200mm), 15¾in (400mm) from each end. This is where you will position the split poles to support the logs or poles that form the riser.

2 Dig two holes about 12in (300mm) deep and set a split pole in each of the holes.

3 Use a carpenter's level across the upper surface of the poles that form each riser to check that they are level. Even if the ground slopes very slightly, you may need to dig away some of the soil to ensure that the first pole is absolutely horizontal. If the ground is very uneven, you will have to excavate a level foundation.

4 Temporarily remove the horizontal pole and check that the split poles are vertical. Then gradually fill the holes around them with soil. Use one of the poles to compact the soil every 4in (100mm) or so.

5 Reposition the first pole, double-checking that it is level. Position a second pole on top of the first to complete the front of the riser. Use humps of soil at each end to keep the poles in place. Check that the two poles are still level and gradually bank soil up against the entire length of the riser.

6 Measure 3¼ft (1m) back from the center of the logs towards the slope. This is the depth of the riser and may vary according to the slope and the dimensions of your own steps. Knock a peg into the ground at this point. Do the same at the other end of the step.

7 Repeat Steps 1–6 and, as you dig into the bank, backfill between the risers. If yours is a very shallow slope, you will need to fill with soil from other parts of the garden. Do the same for each of the risers, using a pole to compact the soil between them.

8 There are many ways to retain soil at the sides of the steps: with a rock garden, by planting, or by nailing split poles between the risers. Because of the slope, the shorter 21⅔in (550mm) split pole is nailed to the bottom pole of the riser; then the 3½ft (1.1m) split pole is nailed into place.

RUSTIC SCREEN

A SIMPLE SCREEN — made from treated poles and straight, stripped saplings, round laths or cane — is both visually effective and practical, particularly in a small, informal garden. It can be used to shield an area from public view; to hide garbage containers, a compost heap or other unsightly but necessary clutter; or, more romantically, to help set the style of your garden.

1 WEEKEND

YOU WILL NEED

TOOLS

- shovel and/or spade
- tape measure
- carpenter'slevel
- tenon saw
- hammer
- drill, with a bit to match the size of your screws
- screwdriver

MATERIALS

- concrete: 2½lbs (1.2kg) cement; 10¼lbs (4.65kg) sand; 10¼lbs (4.65kg) crushed stone or 2656lbs (120kg) ready-mixed materials
- poles: 3 poles x 8ft x 3½in (2.4m x 90mm)
- laths: 75–80 laths x 6ft x 1½–1¾in (1.8m x 30–45mm)
- wire nails: 8 nails x 4in (100mm)
- anodized screws: 150–160 screws x 2in (50mm) (2 per lath used)

OUT OF SIGHT, OUT OF MIND

This rustic screen may be built to any shape, angled or straight, and may be freestanding or attached at one end to an existing wall. Materials specified here are for an L-shaped screen designed to shield a corner adjacent to the house. The two lengths that make up the L are 6ft (1.8m) and 4ft (1.2m) long, giving a total screen length of 10ft (3m) if you prefer to build it as a straight structure. Split poles are used for horizontal supports, to which the round, rustic laths are securely screwed. If laths are not available, cane or bamboo could be substituted.

Decide where the screen is to be located, but before you start digging foundation footings, determine where underground pipes and drains are located and avoid these. Level and remove grass, rocks and stones before you start working. Remember that laths should be affixed above the surface of the ground and the ends of any untreated poles to be anchored in the ground should be coated with a suitable preservative (*see page 166*).

TIP The deeper your footing, the more stable the screen, but this does not mean you have to fill the entire hole with concrete. If a 23½in (600mm) footing is half filled with concrete and then topped up with well-compacted earth, you will easily be able to plant alongside the screen.

1 Measure and mark the position of the screen, ensuring that the corner of the L is square. Mark the position of the three upright poles that will support the screen. If the screen is to be set adjacent to the house or an existing fence or wall, position the nearest pole 15¾in (400mm) in from the structure. Use chalk, white cement, lime or flour to identify the foundation areas, each of which should measure at least 10in x 10in (250mm x 250mm). Dig to a depth of 23½in (600mm).

2 Set the three poles in place in the center of each footing and brace with wooden battens or any other available wood. Use a carpenter's level to check that the poles are absolutely vertical.

3 Mix the cement, sand and crushed stone with sufficient water in a wheelbarrow or on a flat, clean surface. Dampen the earth in each hole and then shovel the concrete mix around each pole to a height of about 10in (250mm) and tamp down well to compact and expel all air bubbles. Before the concrete sets, double-check that the poles are still vertical. Leave overnight and then fill the holes with well-compacted earth.

4 Remove the bracing before nailing the split poles to the upright poles so that they form horizontal supports for the laths. Affix these at the top of the poles and approximately 4in (100mm) above the level of the ground, using a carpenter's level to make certain that they are indeed straight and level. If they are not level, your screen will appear lopsided and you will, in all probability, have to start again.

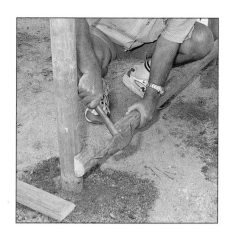

5 Nail all horizontal supports to the uprights, top and bottom, so the wood does not split. The top of each pole should align with the upper edge of the horizontal split poles. If you have not positioned and dug the footings accurately, the upright poles may not align, in which case you should saw off any section of pole that extends above the structure.

6 Since the stripped saplings are never absolutely straight and tend to split easily, it is a good idea to buy laths that are slightly longer than that required. Cut to size by trimming off any split ends and awkward bends. You will then be able to use some of these off-cuts elsewhere in the garden – arranged around flower beds, for instance.

7 Measure and mark where you will screw each of the laths to the screen framework – about 4¾in (120mm) from the top and 3in (80mm) from the bottom – and pre-drill every piece. The position of the horizontal timber will determine the position of the screws. Double-check this before drilling. As this timber tapers, alternate thick and thin top ends.

8 Starting from the outside corner of the structure, screw the laths to the framework so that the top is about 4in (100mm) higher than the upper cross piece. To make the task easier, as you work, mark the position of each screw on the split poles and pre-drill before screwing.

9 Continue working systematically until the screen is complete. Once the laths are all in place, you may want to plant alongside the screen for even greater privacy, and to soften the rather harsh lines of the timber structure.

PICKET FENCE & GATE

ATTENTION TO DETAIL is what makes this attractive picket fence stand out from the rest. Made in the traditional way, with perfectly spaced, pointed pales, it features small round cut-outs at the top of each one.

1 WEEKEND

YOU WILL NEED

TOOLS
- shovel and/or spade
- builder's line or string
- pegs or chalk
- wheelbarrow
- tape measure
- carpenter's level
- paint brushes
- carpenter's square
- pencil
- claw hammer
- screwdriver
- jigsaw, fitted with a standard blade
- drill, with various wood bits

MATERIALS
- concrete: 128lbs (58kg) cement; 507lbs (230kg) sand; 507lbs (230kg) crushed stone
- bitumen: ¼gal (1*l*)
- posts: 4 posts x 5ft x 4in x 1½in (1.5m x 100mm x 40mm)
- pales: 32 pales x 4ft x 2¾in x ¾in (1.2m x 70mm x 20mm), cut from 16 PAR lengths x 8ft (2.4m)
- support rails: 2 rails x 7ft x 2¾in x ¾in (2.1m x 70mm x 20mm); 2 rails x 4ft x 2¾in x ¾in (1.2m x 70mm x 20mm)
- Z-brace: 2 braces x 3¼ft x 2¾in x ¾in (1m x 70mm x 20mm); 1 brace x 3½ft x 2¾in x ¾in (1.1m x 70mm x 20mm) cut at an angle at each end to form the center of the Z
- galvanized nails: 132 nails x 2in (50mm); 8 nails x 3in (75mm)
- galvanized hinges: 2
- anodized screws: 16 screws x ⅛in x ⅝in (3.5mm x 16mm) (for hinges); 7 screws x ⅛in x 1⅜in (3.5 mm x 35mm) for Z-brace
- gate latch, with screws or barrel bolt and screws

ALL FENCED IN

Although ready-made picket panels are widely available, this fencing can be easily assembled by anyone with basic carpentry skills. Furthermore, making a picket fence from scratch gives you the opportunity to vary the design to suit your needs and your own garden design. Instead of using pointed pales, you may prefer to round them off, or perhaps create a more elaborate design. While picket fences are traditionally quite low, they may of course be built to any height, and instead of spacing the pales, you may prefer to position them close together for added privacy.

Materials specified are for two sawn and planed picket panels, one 4ft (1.2m) long and the other 7ft (2.1m), with a 3¼ft-wide (1m) gate. You can alter these measurements to suit your own scheme. If you need to use multiple panels, these should all be the same length and should be attached to posts positioned at equal distances from one another. If your panels are longer than 7ft (2.1m), it is advisable to use sturdier horizontal beams for support – at least 2¾in x 1⅛in (70mm x 30mm) instead of 2¾in x ¾in (70mm x 20mm).

1 Measure out the position of the fence, stringing a line from one end to the other to ensure that the upright posts will be aligned. Mark where the upright posts are to be concreted into the ground. The distance between the posts is dictated by the width of the picket panels: 4ft (1.2m) and 7ft (2.1m) centers, with a 3¼ft-wide (1m) space between the two panels to accommodate the gate. Dig 15¾in x 15¾in x 15¾in (400mm x 400mm x 400mm) footings for the posts and set them in position, bracing with scrap timber. Use a carpenter's level to ensure that they are vertical.

2 Mix concrete on a clean, dry surface or in a builder's wheelbarrow. To prevent moisture from the soil being absorbed into the concrete, dampen the soil in the excavated holes before placing the mixture. Before the concrete sets, again check that the posts are vertical. Allow the concrete to set thoroughly, preferably overnight, before securing the picket panels.

3 To make the pales, measure and mark the central point of each 8ft (2.4m) plank — 4ft (1.2m) from each end and 1⅜in (35mm) from the outside edges. Then, using the 45-degree diagonal on a carpenter's square as a guide, draw two diagonal lines so that they intersect at the central point. This will give you accurate cutting lines.

4 With the jigsaw, cut along the two diagonal lines you have already drawn. Work on a portable workbench or secure a pair of trestles and be sure to hold the wood steady and to cut it firmly.

5 Mark the point at which you want to create the circular cutout effect. This one is centered, 2in (50mm) from the point of the pale. Drill a hole using a flat 1⅛in (30mm) wood bit (bigger if you want to create a larger hole).

6 Mark the position of the 2¾in-wide (70mm) pales on all four cross rails, allowing for a 2¾in-wide (70mm) gap between each. This will make it quicker and easier to construct the panels. Alternatively, since the gap between the pales is the same width as the wood, you use one of the pales as a spacer.

7 Mark the position of the cross pieces on the first pale, 12in (300mm) from the bottom and 8in (200mm) from the top. Position the first pale and check that it is at 90 degrees to the cross pieces.

8 Nail the first pale to the cross piece with four 2in (50mm) nails, two into each cross piece. Leave a 2¾in (70mm) gap as marked and position the next pale. Nail as before. Repeat until each panel is complete.

9 Make the gate in exactly the same way as you assembled the two panels, but with the addition of an extra length of wood from corner to corner to form a Z, which will brace it. Once the two cross pieces have been nailed into place, lay the brace loosely in place and mark the angles of each end of the Z. Cut the ends and then screw the center of the Z to each of the pales.

10 Nail the first panel to the upright posts, 2–4in (50–100mm) off the ground. Use bricks or offcuts of wood to support the base of the fence panels while you work. Check with a carpenter's level to ensure that the cross pieces of each panel are properly aligned with one another; for accuracy, mark their position with a pencil.

11 Using the pencil mark as a guide, nail the second picket panel to the upright posts.

12 Mark the position of the gate hinges on the Z-brace and then use a suitable wood bit to drill the required holes. Screw the hinges to the gate and then attach them to the upright posts, once again using bricks or offcuts of wood to prop up the gate while you work. Use the level vertically to check that the gate is straight. Finally, fit a latch or barrel bolt.

179

BENTWOOD ARCH

THE MATERIALS FOR this attractive, inexpensive bentwood arch could be growing in your own garden. Made from saplings and young, green willow branches, it will blend with the environment, even before it is covered with climbing or creeping plants. Constructed at the top of a flight of garden steps, at the start of a path or as an entrance to an enclosed patio, this arch will immediately add quaint character to your garden.

2–3 HOURS

YOU WILL NEED

TOOLS
- stonemason's hammer
- hacksaw
- pliers or wire cutters

MATERIALS
- metal rods: 4 rods x 4ft (1.2m)
- main frame: 4 stout, straight saplings x 11½–13ft (3.5–4m)
- circles: willow withes
- wire: 1 roll

BEAUTIFULLY BENT

The materials used for this charming arch, which will cover an area of about 4ft x 20in (1.2m x 500mm), may not be found in regular building supply stores. Made with bent wattle saplings and willow withes, which are tied in circles and wired to the wattle mainframe, it is thus a project that relies on what is available in your garden, or the gardens of friends and relatives. If these trees do not grow in your area, use any other young, pliable stems and branches accessible to you. Tough metal rods have been used to support the wattle mainframe so that holes do not have to be dug into the lawn. Laths or small poles could, however, be used instead, provided that they are set well into the ground and the earth around them is thoroughly compacted so that they do not shift.

Make sure that you are absolutely ready with all the tools and materials required for the project before you cut the wood; the more it dries, the more brittle it becomes. If set in place while green, it will retain its shape as it gradually dries out.

TIP Long, thin saplings are easier to bend than thick, stubby ones. These, however, should not be too green or they will simply break as you try to bend them.

1 Decide where you want the arch and then use a stonemason's hammer to knock a metal rod into the ground, so that only about 27½in (700mm) is still above ground.

2 Knock the second rod into the ground, 20in (500mm) away from the first one.

3 The span of the arch will depend on the width of your path or entrance. Make sure that the two rods on the opposite side are positioned square and are equidistant. These are 4ft (1.2m) from the rods on the other side. Double check that they are square by measuring across the diagonal, making sure that both lengths are exactly the same.

4 Remove all branches and leaves from the saplings and saw the ends off all four to ensure they are all the same length.

5 Lay the tapered ends of two saplings together, overlapping by about 3¼ft (1m). Wire the two together in at least three places. Repeat this procedure with the other two saplings.

6 Using wire, secure one end of the joined sapling length to one of the rods and trim the sharp ends. Carefully bend the wood and secure to the rod on the side diagonally opposite. Repeat with the second length of joined sapling.

7 Where the two sections of the mainframe overlap at the apex, join securely with wire.

8 Make rings with willow withes. If the young willow branch is long enough, you may need only one length to make a circle. If they are shorter, interweave two — or even three. Make one circle at a time and check the size as you work. As you get closer to the apex, the rings should become smaller and smaller.

9 Wire the first ring to the sides of the main uprights. Then wire the second circle to the first ring as well as to the framework of the arch.

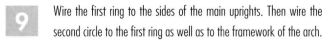

RUSTIC GARDEN BENCH

THIS RUSTIC GARDEN bench makes an attractive addition to an informal garden. Made from relatively rough but treated poles and laths, it is simply screwed together to create a feature that may also be used for seating. Set in the garden or on a patio, it is as decorative as it is useful. The secret is to pre-cut and pre-drill all the lengths required and to ensure that these are all accurately measured.

YOU WILL NEED

TOOLS

- handsaw
- tape measure
- chisel
- hammer
- drill, with various bits
- wrench
- screwdriver
- angle grinder or belt sander

MATERIALS

- poles: 2 poles x 35½in (900mm); 2 poles x 17¾in (450mm); 2 poles x 15¾in (400mm) cut from 2 x 6ft x 2¾–3½in (1.8m x 70–90mm)
- laths: 9 laths x 4ft x 1⅕–1¾in (1.2m x 30–45mm); 5 laths x 3¼ft x 1⅕–1¾in (1m x 30–45mm); 2 laths x 33½in x ⅖–1in (850mm x 10–25mm); 4 laths x 4ft x ⅖–1in (1.25m x 10–25mm); 2 laths x 21⅔in x ⅖–1in (550mm x 10–25mm); 2 laths x 20in x ⅖–1in (500mm x 10–25mm)
- carpenter's pencil
- wood glue
- coach bolts: 4 bolts x ⅖in x ⅗in (10mm x 15 mm), with washers
- chipboard screws: 10 screws x 2⅓in (60mm)

5–6 HOURS

REST IN STYLE

Basic carpentry skills will enable you to construct this garden bench from poles and laths in just a few hours. Laths are available in various thicknesses, although they are never entirely regular. However, it is their irregular nature that adds charm to this rustic outdoor furniture.

The rustic garden bench is an ideal project for the beginner carpenter as there are no joints to worry about and this design could even be nailed together – but do not be tempted to take the easy route. By taking just a little more time and making an extra effort by screwing the bench together, the finished item will not only look more professional, it will also last a lot longer.

Once you are confident about your woodworking skills, you can adapt this design and create your own homemade furniture.

TIP Before screwing the laths to the leg framework, drill pilot holes. This will make screwing the bench together a lot easier.

1 First assemble the two outer ends of the bench, including the legs, to create an h-shape for each side. Use the 35½in (900mm) and 15¾in (400mm) poles for the legs, measuring 15in (380mm) from the bottom of each to accommodate the connecting piece. Mark where the connecting piece will be situated with a pencil. Cut and chisel out a notch in the pole approximately ⅗–¾in (15–20mm) deep and the width of the pole (2¾–3½in/70–90mm).

2 Drill a ¼in (6mm) pilot hole in the center of each end of the 17¾in (450mm) poles. Using a flat wood bit, drill about ⅛in (5mm) into the lengths at the point where they are to join the 17¾in (450mm) cross pieces. This hole will create a recess for the bolthead. Change the drill bit and drill a ⅜in (10mm) hole all the way through the wood. Put a generous amount of wood glue onto each of the notches and slot the three pieces of wood together. Use a wrench to bolt it together. Repeat for the second side.

3 Use an angle grinder or belt sander to smooth the ends of the poles. It would probably be easier to do this only once the bench has been partly assembled, but you could also smooth the ends before you start working. Set the legs upright and assemble the seat by screwing six 4ft (1.2m) laths across the width of the bench. Be absolutely sure to keep the bench perfectly square.

4 Turn the bench on its side and position two of the 4ft (1.25m) lengths from corner to corner to form a cross brace approximately 1¾in (45mm) below the seat. Screw these to the inside of the legs. Then screw the two 20in-long (500mm) laths to the inside of the legs between the cross brace and the seat. Screw the last lath to the seat, in front of the leg. Screw a 3¼ft-long (1m) lath to the 20in (500mm) laths affixed on each side.

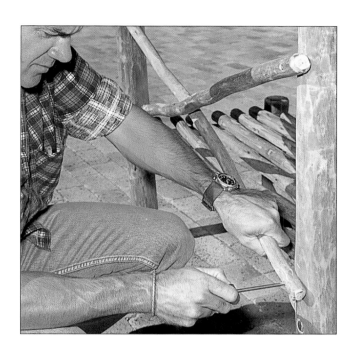

5 Use two more of the 4ft (1.25m) laths to form a cross piece at the back of the bench and screw to secure. This will stabilize the seat and make it more sturdy.

6 Screw the two 21½in (550mm) laths in place. The top of each is screwed to the back cross piece (*see Step 5*) and to the front of the back lath in the seat.

7 Assemble the back of the bench, using 4ft (1.2m) laths at the base and four shorter 3¼ft (1m) laths at the top.

8 Screw the two decorative 33½in (850mm) laths to the framework on the outside of the legs.

TRELLIS ARBOR

A CHARMING ARBOR, designed to fulfil the traditional function of supporting vines and climbing plants, is an understated feature in a spacious garden. Set under a well-established willow tree, it provides a comforting place to sit out of the sun or just to read, ponder or dream. This design is, however, not limited to the larger garden; it would be equally at home in the smallest area, tucked away beside a flower garden, perhaps smothered with climbing roses or jasmine.

YOU WILL NEED

TOOLS

- spade
- tape measure
- builder's square
- carpenter's level
- hammer
- drill, with a suitable wood bit
- wrenches
- paint brush

MATERIALS

- beams: 2 beams x 9½ft x 5¾in x 1¼in (2.9m x 146mm x 32mm), cut at an angle at each end
- uprights: 4 uprights x 8½ft x 5¾in x 1¼in (2.6m x 146mm x 32mm)
- bracing lengths: 4 lengths x 5¾in x 5¾in (146mm x 146mm), with one end cut at a 45-degree angle
- crosspieces: 2 lengths x 35½in x 5¾in x 1¼in (900mm x 146mm x 32mm); 2 lengths x 35½in x 3in x 1¼in (900mm x 75mm x 32mm);1 length x 6½ft x 3in x 1¼in (2m x 75mm x 32mm)
- trellis: 2 lengths x 71½in x 1¼in x ⅝in (1810mm x 32mm x 16mm); 2 lengths x 6½ft x 1¼in x ⅝in (2m x 32mm x 16mm); 2 lengths x 65in x 1¼in x ⅝in (1650mm x 32mm x 16mm); 4 lengths x 35½ft x 1¼in x ⅝in (900mm x 32mm x 16mm); 2 lengths x 5¾in x 1¼in x ⅝in (146mm x 32mm x 16mm)
- cuphead bolts: 22 bolts x ⅛in x 3in (8mm x 75mm)
- galvanized wire nails: 82 nails x 2in (50mm); 4 nails x 5⅛in (130mm); 4 nails x 7in (175mm)
- paint: primer/undercoat and a top coat

1 WEEKEND

OF SHADE AND SHELTER

An arbor is one of the oldest garden features, said to date back to well-designed gardens of ancient Egypt. In its purist form, arbors incorporate a place to sit, which is sheltered by plants growing on a frame, and this trellis arbor draws its inspiration from these traditional structures.

Cut wood has been used for this project, and it has been painted white to create a contrast within the foliage. Very open trelliswork provides a framework for planting. Additional slats may be used to create a slightly closer-knit trellis or even a lattice effect.

Very basic carpentry skills are required to complete this project. An electric drill is an essential tool and a circular saw is recommended. The wood may, however, be cut using a handsaw.

1 Cut all the timber to size and coat with a suitable primer or undercoat. Allow to dry overnight. Working on a flat, level surface, lay one timber beam out with two of the timber uprights. Position the uprights 17¾in (450mm) from each end and use a square to check that the two lengths of timber meet at right angles.

2 Drill two pilot holes through the upright and through the beam, where the two lengths of wood cross each other. It wil also help if you clamp them together.

3 Before tightening the cuphead bolts, check that the joins are absolutely square by using the 3:4:5 method (*see page 163*). Here the dimensions used to check for square are 12in (300mm), 15¾in (400mm)and, across the corner, 20in (500mm).

4 Once all four bolts have been tightened, with nuts and washers in place, brace the uprights to the beams on both sides. Use three of the 2in (50mm) nails to secure the timber brace to the top of the upright, then drill two pilot holes at each corner and nail two of the longer 5⅛in (130mm) and 7in (175mm) nails at an angle through the wood. Repeat the process with the other beam and uprights.

5 Dig 23⅝in-deep (600mm) footings for the four upright posts and position the first section of the framework. Use a carpenter's level to check that the beam is straight and level.

6 You will need help to properly align the two sections. Check and double-check with a carpenter's level on all surfaces, both horizontal and vertical, before refilling and compacting soil in the footings. Brace temporarily with two slats on each side.

7 Once the structure is straight, level and plumb, bolt the side timbers into place. Start at the top on one side and then move to the top on the other side, each time drilling pilot holes before attempting to secure with a wrench. Make sure that the cross pieces are flush with the beams and that the upright timbers remain absolutely vertical. Bolt the thinner (3in/75mm) cross pieces to the uprights – 8in (200mm) from the base – using one bolt at each end instead of two; then bolt the longer 3in (75mm) length to the base at the back of the structure, in line with the two side timbers.

8 Remove the bracing and nail the trellis to the framework, spacing evenly and using two wire nails at each end. Centre the two 65in (1650mm) slats at each side and use the two longest lengths at the back, spacing evenly with two 5¾in-long (146mm) spacers against the outside of the beam to align the trellis. Nail the horizontal trellis at the back of the arbor with a space of 21¼in (540mm) from the beam to the first slat, allowing for the same space between the first and second and second and third slats. Line up side slats with those at the back of the structure.

PRACTICAL PLAY FRAME

A GARDEN PLAY frame can bring a great deal of pleasure to children of all ages. Designed with swings, slides, nets, rope ladders, platforms and even forts and hide-outs, it will keep little people occupied for hours. This design is relatively simple and incorporates a slide and two tire swings, as well as an open platform accessed by a wooden ladder.

1 WEEKEND

YOU WILL NEED

TOOLS
- spade and/or shovel
- tape measure
- builder's square
- carpenter's level
- hammer
- drill, with various bits
- wrenches

MATERIALS
- deck: 2 lengths x 31½in x 3½in (800mm x 90mm) poles; 7 planks x 31½in x 4½in x 1½in (800mm x 114mm x 38mm)
- deck support structure: 4 lengths x 10ft x 4⅓in (3m x 110mm) poles
- Swing frame: 2 beams x 12ft x 3½in (3.6m x 90mm); 1 beam x 10ft x 5in (3m x 125mm)
- rails: 2 rails x 3⅓ft x 2in (1m x 50mm)
- ladder: 2 lengths x 8ft x 3in (2.4m x 75mm), with 6 holes machined 4in (100mm) from one end and at 15¾in (400mm) intervals; 6 lengths x 23⅔in x 2in (600mm x 50mm)
- swing: 2 old tires; 2 galvanized strapping x 1½in x 6⅓in (40mm x 160mm) ; 2 D-rings; 4 chains x 57in (1450mm); 4 swing fittings with bolts
- slide: 10ft (3m) fiberglass, with all fittings
- self-tapping screws: 28 screws x 4in (100mm)
- steel nails: 10 galvanized nails x 6in (150mm)
- cuphead bolts: 5 bolts x ½in x 7¾in (12mm x 200mm); 1 bolt x ½in x 7in (12mm x 180mm); 1 bolt x ½in x 9in (12mm x 230mm)
- wax oil or wood sealer

PLAY TIME

Play structures may be as simple or as elaborate as you wish, and will depend on the space you have in your garden and the needs of the children who will use it.

These tire swings can be made by cutting all but 23⅔in (600mm) of the central tread from the tire and turning it inside out before attaching galvanized strapping to the top of each cut end. D-rings are attached to the strapping and a chain to the rings.

For the ladder, use two machined poles to accommodate six 2in (50mm) rungs at 15¾in (400mm) centers.

Safety is paramount. Use round, factory-prepared poles that will not splinter, and make sure the entire structure is solid and secure. If the soil in your garden is unstable, set the posts in concrete. Grass makes a good surface under the play frame; if grass does not grow well in your garden, consider using crushed bark instead. Never use gravel, as it invites cuts and grazes.

Since the poles are cumbersome and heavy, you will need at least one person to help you with the building of the play frame structure.

1 A certain amount of work can be done well before the frame is erected on site. For instance, seal all the poles with wax oil or wood sealer before construction begins.

2 Make the deck by fixing the seven planks to the two 31½in-long (800mm) poles with ripping screws. If you want to leave a slight gap between the planks, saw one of the planks in half, or use a different dimension timber. Check the corners with a square to ensure they are at 90 degrees. Place the deck on the ground and mark all four corners. Dig 23⅔in-deep (600mm) foundation footings at each corner.

3 Position the upright poles and use a carpenter's level to check that they are perfectly straight.

4 Hold each pole steady as a helper fills in around them with hardcore and soil, and compact well. Fill the hole little by little to ensure the soil around each one is properly compacted.

5 Position the deck 5ft (1.5m) from the ground and nail it temporarily in place from underneath.

6 Using a flat wood bit, drill through each upright pole, into the horizontal poles supporting the decking. Then use a countersunk bit to create a recess for the bolthead.

7 Using a wrench, tighten the four bolts you have inserted into the uprights and cross pieces.

8 Dig two holes 31½in (800mm) from two adjacent poles supporting the deck. These are to accommodate the ladder. If you are using poles that have been machined to accommodate the rungs, the ladder is easily assembled by simply knocking the 2in (50mm) poles into the machined holes. Position the ladder so that the top rests against the deck and then secure them with galvanized wire nails.

9 Attach the four swing fittings to the 10ft-long (3m) swing beam, 20in (500mm) apart.

10 If you are assembling your own tire swings, use a steel bit to drill holes for the galvanized strapping and make three holes in each swing seat for drainage.

11 Dig two more holes, 10ft (3m) apart and 10ft (3m) from the deck, for the swing's A-frame. Mark and dig 23⅝in (600mm) foundations for the A-frame poles. Bolt the A-frame poles together, about 10in (250mm) from the top, using the 7in (180mm) cuphead bolt. You will need help to position and support these poles in the footings while you check they are straight. Fill the holes with earth and compact (as in Step 4). Place the 10ft (3m) swing beam across the apex and position it on the second pole, and about 2in (50mm) from the top of the pole. Use the largest bolt to secure the swing beam to the deck before attaching the swing.

12 Nail the two rails to the upright poles, 20in (500mm) from the bottom of the deck. Finally, fix the slide in position according to the manufacturer's instructions.

TREEHOUSE

EVERY CHILD LONGS to have a treehouse. Set in the branches of two established pine trees, this hideaway has been clad with offcuts of pine, still clad with the bark. The treehouse has a solid pine floor and a marine-grade plywood roof, and is sheltered from the elements. Since it is built around a pole framework, it can be built as a freestanding structure, perhaps alongside recently planted saplings that will grow and envelop the treehouse.

3 WEEKENDS

YOU WILL NEED

TOOLS
- carpenter's level
- hammer
- drill, with flat wood bits
- wrench
- circular saw

MATERIALS
- poles: 2 poles x 12ft x 3½in (3.6m x 90mm); 4 poles x 6ft x 3½in (1.8m x 90mm)
- split poles: 4 poles x 4½ft x 3½in (1.4m x 90mm); 4 poles x 5½ft x 3½in (1.7m x 90mm); 2 poles x 6¼ft x 3½in (1.9m x 90mm); 2 poles x 5¼ft x 3½in (1.6m x 90mm); 2 poles x 6ft x 3½in (1.8m x 90mm); 2 poles x 7½ft x 3½in (2.3m x 90mm)
- rough wood: 2 lengths x 6ft x 4in x 1½in (1.8m x 100mm x 40mm); 1 length x 7¼ft x 3in x 1½in (2.2m x 80mm x 40mm)
- floorboards: 36 boards x 29⅓in x 4in x 1in (745mm x 100mm x 25mm); 18 boards x 27½in x 4in x 1in (700mm x 100mm x 25mm)
- siding: 36 lengths x 7½ft x 4in
- x ½–1½in (2.3m x 100mm x 10–40mm); 34 lengths x 6ft x 4in x ½–1½in (1.8m x 100mm x 10–40mm)
- heavy-gauge brackets: 4 brackets x 4in x 4in x 2in (100mm x 100mm x 50mm); 4 brackets x 3in x 3in x 2in (75mm x 75mm x 50mm); 4 brackets x 2in x 2in x ¾in (50mm x 50mm x 20mm)
- coach screws: 20 screws x ⅜in x 3in (10mm x 75mm)
- cuphead bolts: 16 bolts x ¼in x 2in (6mm x 50mm)
- galvanized wire nails: 24 nails x 5in (125mm); 368 nails x 3in (75mm)
- clout nails: 70 nails x 1½in (40mm)
- fibercement: 2 sheets x 7½ft x 4ft x ⅜in (2.3m x 1.2m x 10mm)
- roof paint

HIGH IN THE SKY

This treehouse can be built in a series of weekends and because it is mostly nailed together, older children can help.

The dimensions may be altered to fit your location. You need two large trees growing 6½–8ft (2–2.5m) apart, but the structure must have sufficient support and be accessible to children. This one is 8ft (2.5m) above ground, between trees growing 7¼ft (2.2m) apart.

Solid poles acts as supports, but the type of beams and siding is optional. The roof covering used here is marine-grade plywood sheeting. Tough marine plywood, made for use on sailing vessels, is an ideal option, but it is more expensive.

Two windows and a door have been incorporated into this design. These may be left as open spaces or you can make a solid door and hinged shutters for the windows from the siding cut from these areas. For the not-so-nimble to gain access, a ladder of sorts is essential. While an ordinary wooden ladder will do the job, a permanent step ladder is more appealing and child-friendly. Alternatively, provide the young tenants with a rope ladder that can be dragged inside while they are in residence.

1 Secure two 12ft-long (3.6m) poles between the two trees to act as support beams. Nail the first one temporarily in place, using a level to make certain that it is straight and level. Now nail the second beam in place, ensuring that it is level with the first one.

2 Use the 4in x 4in (100mm x 100mm) brackets and coach screws to secure the poles to the trees. Secure to the tree with two screws and to the pole with one screw, bending the bracket to accommodate the curve of the pole.

3 The four 6ft (1.8m) poles are now bolted at right angles across the top of the two support beams. Use a ⅓in (10mm) flat wood bit to drill through to the beams. Now fasten the two end cross beams onto the support beams using the cuphead bolts.

4 To strengthen the support structure, nail a V-brace to the tree and the end cross beam on both sides. Use the four 4½ft (1.4m) split poles, and cut off each end at an angle before nailing into place with the longer nails. As an additional precaution, nail two of the 5½ft (1.7m) split poles to form a brace from the outside end of each pole to the tree.

5 Bolt the other two cross beams into place. The distance between the cross beams you have already bolted should be 7ft (2.1m) and the remaining two beams should be bolted between these, at 27½in (700mm) centers. Now nail the floorboards in place. (The shorter ones are nailed in the middle and the longer ones on each side.)

6 Once the floor is in place, erect the framework for the treehouse itself. You will need the two remaining 5½ft (1.7m) split poles as well as the two 6¼ft (1.9m) lengths. The difference in height will ensure that you have a 8in (200mm) slope for the roof. Position the first corner pole against the end of one of the cross beams, with the flat side facing inwards. Check that it is vertical before nailing with two 5in (125mm) nails. Repeat this process at the other end of the cross beam. Nail the longer split poles to the cross beams on the other side.

7 The 5¼ft (1.6m) split poles are then fixed to the floorboards with 3in (75mm) brackets, between the two 5½ft (1.7m) poles. Make sure that the round side of the pole is facing inwards. The reason for this is that the siding on the longer sides of the tree-house will be fixed to the outside of the structure, while the siding on each side will be fixed to the inside.

8 Affix the 7½ft (2.3m) split poles across the front and back of the structure, at the top of the uprights. Use 2in (50mm) brackets with the smaller coach screws at the corners, and 3in (75mm) nails to join the two center uprights. Tighten the coach screws with a suitable wrench.

9 To complete the top of the framework, affix the 6ft (1.8m) of rough-cut wood to the top at the sides.

10 Nail the siding to the framework, using the 3in (75mm) nails. Start from the floor and work upwards. If you want a door and at least one window, decide between which of the upright posts you want to situate these. Once you have secured the siding, cut the excess wood from the edges of the structure with an electrical circular saw or a handsaw.

11 Before you are able to secure the roof sheeting, you will need to fit a central beam. Screw or nail the 7¼ft (2.2m) length of rough-cut wood into the top of the framework at each side.

12 Finally, nail the roof sheeting on. The two sheets should overlap by 8in (200mm) and have a 4in (100mm) overhang on either side. Secure the lower sheet first so that the higher sheet overlaps it and allows the rain to run away and not into the treehouse. Use the clout nails and nail every 6in (150mm) along all the beams.

This timber structure provides a focal point in a large garden, as well as shade for birdcages.

ACKNOWLEDGMENTS

Do-It-Yourself is a misnomer, especially when it comes to putting a book together on the subject. No author can do it alone! So as authors, we have a huge number of individuals and companies to thank. In particular, Mike Ingram and Rod Taylor of Corobrik, South Africa, who have always done all they can, supplying both bricks and locations, to help us build and create the kind of brick projects that will appeal to DIY readers. Andy van Niekerk of Smartstone is another stalwart who has supplied precast concrete stone slabs and blocks and helped us produce DIY projects on numerous occasions. His internationally available product is featured in the Stone Slab Patio. Fred Brown of Sandstone of the Earth kept his staff working into the Christmas holidays to ensure we could photograph some superior stonework, and we thank him for this. The team at Cerf's also put up with 'interference' so we could shoot them installing the Practical Play Frame. Thank you. Katrine Puttick of G Pots (Hout Bay) and Hendriques (Lanseria) loaned us numerous items both planted and unplanted, out of her shop and from her home. Claire and Rob Starke built (and allowed the construction of) a few projects in their beautiful garden, just so we could complete the book in limited time. Several timber suppliers also came to our rescue and we thank Mike Raubenheimer of Woodline for poles, Leroy of The Pole Yard in Noordhoek, particularly for the superior lathes, and for discovering Bradley Dale who makes amazing rustic lathe furniture. When it came to water features, technical advice was as important as the materials, which are not always so freely available. Thanks to Tony Howell and the team at Kaytech for advice and making geotextiles available. Thanks also to Adriano Swanepoel of Dalven for the superior bitumen waterproofing compound and advise on how to use it. Ken Maund of Specialised Rubber Products also went that extra mile, transporting butyl rubber to the Western Cape in record time. This was used in several of the projects. Andrew Scott of Simply Green was another contractor who happily allowed us to slow down his work for photographic purposes; thank you, your stonework is great. Finally, thank you also to Sundial Exclusives for the loan of one of the world's most stunning sundials (an order, loaned to us for a few days!). Without these people, this book would not be a reality.